the little book of
quick fixes
for a spotless home

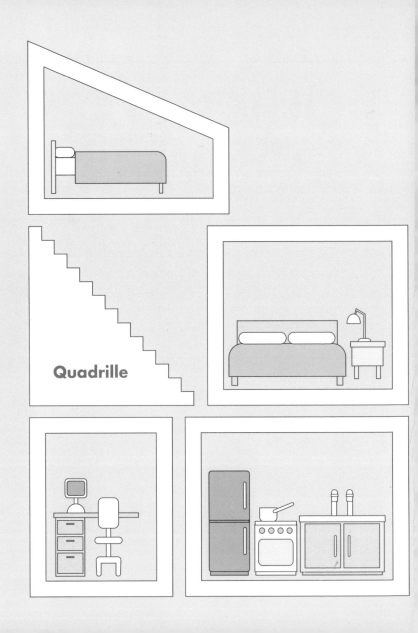

Quadrille

THE LITTLE BOOK OF
QUICK FIXES
FOR A SPOTLESS HOME

**Bridget
Bodoano**

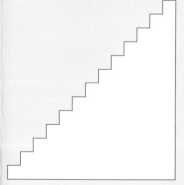

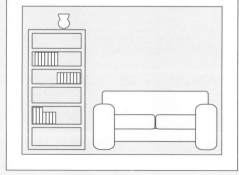

First published in 2006 by
Quadrille Publishing Ltd, Alhambra House,
27–31 Charing Cross Road, London WC2H 0LS

Reprinted in 2006
10 9 8 7 6 5 4 3 2

Editorial Director Jane O'Shea
Creative Director Helen Lewis
Project Editor Lisa Pendreigh
Designer Claire Peters
Illustrator Bridget Bodoano
Production Director Vincent Smith
Production Controller Bridget Fish

Cataloguing in Publication Data: a catalogue record for this book
is available from the British Library.

ISBN-13: 978 184400 281 8
ISBN-10: 1 84400 281 0

Printed in China

Contents

A Question Of Standards

how clean is clean?

On the whole, a clean home is a much nicer place to live for you and your family, partner or housemates. Just how clean is clean depends on your own standards and character, but most of us fall into one of the following categories:

cleanaholic

Pristine perfectionists wipe down surfaces, empty bins and clean sinks, baths and basins on a daily basis. They regularly indulge in deep-cleansing routines, leaving no ornament unturned in their pursuit of dust control. They are also likely to treat ironing as a leisure activity.

clean enough

With less time — or better things to do — these perfectly normal people are more likely to do a good weekly clean rather than daily maintenance. However, any obvious nasties are cleaned up pretty promptly. Will ignore the odd cobweb, but likes a clean floor.

slightly grubby

Not as tuned into dirt and grime as others, the occupants of slightly grubby homes do what they think is basic cleaning, but only tackle what they see. They seldom venture into corners and underneath things, are generally dust-tolerant and don't notice (or care about) the odd stain, dribble and splodge.

complete slob

For reasons known only to themselves, they are oblivious to the fact that cleaning exists. Whether through a lack of education or self-esteem, they are happy to live in squalor until struck down by either conscience or a nasty infection.

Standard Requirements

Even those who think they are clean are
often in dirt-denial, so take off the rose-
tinteds and have a good look around to
check your credentials. If three or more
of the following are present in your home,
it is time to get cleaning:

- an excess of smears, splodges and dribbles, plus rings from mugs and cups
- more than a day's worth of dirty dishes
- more than one piece of mouldy food
- black mould and mildew on walls, tiles or floors
- nasty smells
- areas of unidentifiable stuff, which is gooey, greasy or sticky
- obvious fingermarks
- dust that has a greenish tinge
- large fluff balls (dust bunnies)
- a very dirty hob
- overflowing rubbish bin
- serious dirt around handles, especially fridges
- dark brown stains in sinks, loos, basins and baths
- floors where it is difficult to determine their true colour

I Storecupboard Cheats

Knowing a little of the chemistry of cleaning will help you choose the right products. Whether you opt for the old-fashioned simplicity of bicarbonate of soda and vinegar, the cheap and cheerful proprietary brands or their eco-friendly equivalents, the fact is that both daily and deep cleansing can be carried out very effectively with a relatively small number of products.

Chemistry Lessons

soaps and detergents

Also known as surfactants, they assist in the wetting process by breaking down the surface tension of water, surrounding the dirt molecules and then preventing them from being re-absorbed. Soaps are made from animal or vegetable fats and oils whereas detergents are made from petro-chemicals. Soap is not necessarily milder than detergent, but the fact that the latter are made from petro-chemicals makes soap more eco-friendly. However, soap forms scum that can be a problem especially in hard-water areas.

solvents

The most common and gentle solvent is water; when mixed with soaps and detergents, water can dissolve most forms of dirt. More serious stains and dirt may need stronger solvents. Turpentine and white spirit are used in specialist cleaning products, but as they are potentially hazardous they should be used sparingly and carefully.

acids and alkalis

These do the job of dirt-busting. Their strength is measured in pH, indicated by a number from 0-14. Below pH 7 is considered acidic, pH 7 is neutral, and anything above is alkaline. The further away from neutral they are, the harsher they are, especially on skin. Alkalis work well on grease or oily dirt and so laundry products and kitchen cleaners tend to be alkaline. Acids are good at removing soap scum and hard-water deposits, so most bathroom cleaners are mildly acidic. Acids and alkalis neutralise one another so don't think that using strong forms of both will be doubly effective, in fact they will cancel each other out.

Safety First

All cleaning products are potentially hazardous if they are used incorrectly, ingested or come into contact with skin, so **BE WARNED**.

read labels
Labels contain important information regarding contents, instructions for use, safety warnings and what to do in case of accidents.

follow instructions
Failure to use a product correctly can produce poor results as well as potential damage or a risk to health and safety.

keep safe
Keep all cleaning products out of reach of children and away from food.

do not decant
Leave products in their original containers. As well as having access to the information on the label,

there is less risk of using the wrong product or of someone mistaking it for something else.

use carefully

Strong cleaners often include toxic chemicals and solvents, such as alcohol, which are highly inflammable. Take care to avoid contact with skin, fabrics, carpets and furniture.

use sparingly

Do not exceed stated doses. Using more doesn't necessarily mean a quicker or better result, though instructions on the label may suggest higher amounts in certain circumstances.

bleach alert

Never mix chlorine bleach with any other product. Combined with acids, alkalis, ammonia (and urine), chlorine creates chlorine gas... which kills.

Cleaning Basics

The sight of all those cleaning products on the supermarket shelves is enough to give anyone the vapours. But don't panic. The principles of getting things clean are pretty simple, and a few good basics are all you need. Look at the labels and choose those with the fewest and least scary sounding ingredients, and the least number of warnings and conditions for use.

washing-up liquid

A mild cleanser useful not only for dishes but for many jobs from washing down worktops and paintwork to mopping up or removing stains from fabrics and furniture.

cream cleansers

These contain abrasives that help to remove dirt. The major brands are usually quite gentle and providing you use a non-scratch sponge or cloth can be safely used on most surfaces. For tough jobs use with a scouring cloth or brush, but only on robust surfaces.

multi-purpose cleaner

A cleaning liquid with no abrasives that can be used on all surfaces including sinks, baths and floors. Can be used neat or diluted in water.

chlorine bleach / disinfectant

Chlorine bleach is an effective germ-killer and will dissolve stains and whiten fabrics. When diluted it is safe to use in areas where food is prepared as a general disinfectant. Chlorine bleach is often the germ-killing ingredient in disinfectants, which work in much the same way as household bleach but are formulated for safe use for medicinal purposes. **Remember, don't mix chlorine bleach with any other cleaning materials.**

Green Issues

Concern for the planet and personal health has increased the popularity of eco-friendly cleaning products. Choose to be totally 'green' or opt for a mix of eco and non-eco, where you are 'green' most of the time but use stronger products for tough jobs.

standard cleaning products

- they are very effective
- they are fast acting
- they are often cheaper than eco-alternatives

- they can contain highly toxic and corrosive chemicals
- the processes involved in their manufacture can cause pollution
- too many chemicals are being flushed into the water system causing pollution
- chemicals in cleaners are linked to allergic reactions, including asthma

eco-friendly products

• they use more environmentally-friendly ingredients and production
• natural ingredients are bio-degradable and therefore better for the sewage and water-supply systems
• they are safer and less toxic (though natural products can be dangerous in high doses)
• they are less likely to irritate skin and usually smell nice
• they are less likely to provoke allergic reactions

• some are less effective than standard equivalents
• they are normally more expensive than standard equivalents

Green Chemistry

You can concoct your own eco-friendly homemade cleansers from simple, inexpensive ingredients. Some are readily available in supermarkets or DIY stores but you may have to ask for others at a pharmacy or specialist shop. They may not be quite as efficient as their modern, chemically laden alternatives so you may need to clean more frequently, allow more time for them to work and use more elbow grease.

green chemistry set
• **soap** (surfactant) – eco-friendly washing-up liquid
• **solvents** – water mostly, but use turpentine, white spirit or eucalyptus oil for heavy-duty oil and grease
• **acids** – white vinegar, lemon juice, carbonated water
• **alkalis** – bicarbonate of soda, borax, washing soda
• **natural disinfectants** – white vinegar, lemon juice, tea tree oil, eucalyptus oil

Green Ingredients

vinegar

Vinegar is the product of choice amongst the cleaning intelligentsia. It is an acid and is very versatile. As well as being delicious on chips, it's a good dirt buster and is brilliant for dissolving limescale. It is also a natural and very safe disinfectant. Any vinegar will perform these tasks but distilled white vinegar is best. It can be used undiluted for stains and tough limescale or diluted with water.

lemon juice

An acid that cuts through grease. Fresh lemons are best and you can also use the squeezed halves to wipe over surfaces to clean and disinfect.

bicarbonate of soda
(sodium bicarbonate)

Readily available in supermarkets it is an alkali and a versatile cleaner. Can be used neat on its own or dissolved in water or vinegar and can be made into a paste. Reacts with water or vinegar to produce a bit of fizz to speed up the cleaning process.

borax

A non-toxic alkali, available as a white crystaline powder, it disinfects, bleaches and deodorises. Also an effective insecticide and fungicide.

washing soda
(sodium carbonate)

A mild alkali sold in crystal form, it can be used as a general cleaner, is a good stain remover and is useful for unblocking drains.

5 Simple Solutions

Despite the plethora of cleaning materials on the market these basic cleaning solutions are good enough for day-to-day use on everyday, not-too-tough dirt.

Hot water with a squeeze of washing-up liquid is a good all-purpose wiper and washer-down.

Put a solution of 1 part vinegar to 1 part water in a spray bottle and use as a general-purpose cleaner for work-surfaces, tiles and sinks.

Make a mild abrasive cleaner by adding a few drops of water to bicarbonate of soda to form a paste.

20ml of household bleach in 5 litres of water makes a good disinfectant for wiping down surfaces, washing out rubbish bins or soaking items such as brushes and combs.

4 tablespoons of bicarbonate of soda in 1 litre of warm water is good for wiping out fridges and ovens.

Well Oiled

Make the most of the nourishing and moisturising properties of oil in your cleaning routines.

olive oil

A dab on a duster brings a sheen to wood as well as picking up more dirt, alternatively mix vinegar and olive oil in equal parts for a more thorough job.

P.S. Don't use your best extra-virgin, go for something more refined or opt for sunflower oil.

baby oil

If your trendy stainless steel splashback, fridge or cooker is looking a bit streaky try a little baby oil on a lint-free cloth.

For a more polished finish on vinyl and linoleum add a capful of baby oil to the cleaning water.

danish oil and finishing oil

These thinner, easy-to-use oils are used for treating or re-juvenating wooden floors, worktops and furniture. They can be used on a more regular basis as part of the cleaning process to add extra nourishment and increase water resistance. Use sparingly on a clean, lint-free cloth and buff off any excess.

Stain Stand-By Kit

Swift action is always advisable to prevent spills and splashes from damaging surfaces, furnishings and clothing. Make sure you have a few basic ingredients in stock at all times to cope with emergencies.

- **carbonated water** or club soda (soda water)
- **mild washing-up liquid** – the eco-friendly ones are mild and non-coloured
- **sponges** and clean cloths – a generous pile of absorbent cloths for mopping up and drying, old cut up sheets, towels and t-shirts are good for this
- **neutralisers** – water, milk, sugar water, salt water
- **white spirit** – useful for spillages of substances with non-water solvents such as gloss paint, oils and glues
- **biological laundry detergent** – for more stubborn stains

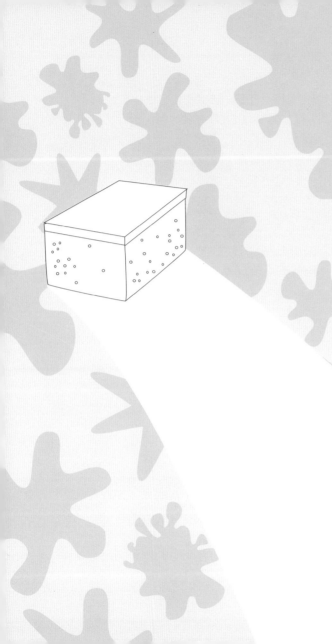

Stain First-Aid

blot

Blot up all excess liquid using a good supply of cloths or sponges. Keep going until all excess moisture has been absorbed.

dilute and disperse

Dilute and disperse any stain with a bubbly liquid — carbonated water or club soda are best.

dab

Blot up any excess liquid by dabbing with a clean, dry cloth.

rub

Rub the stain with cloths or sponges dipped in a mild solution of washing-up liquid. Always work inwards from the outside to avoid spreading the stained area. For trickier, darker stains apply a little biological laundry detergent and leave for a while.

rinse

Rinse using clean cloths or a sponge and clean water.

dry

Dry as much as possible by dabbing and blotting with clean, dry cloths.

treat

If necessary, treat any remaining stain with a purpose-made stain remover but remember to read the instructions carefully. Sometimes it is necessary to let the stain dry before treatment.

2 Tools of the Trade

You are more likely to be inspired to get on with the cleaning if you have the right tools. Basic cleaning equipment is mostly cheap and, with all those bright colours, cheerful enough to turn a chore into pleasure.

Basic Cleaning Kit

- floor mop
- mop-bucket
- broom with fine bristles
- collection of scourers
- dustpan and brush
- cotton dishcloths (minimum of 4)
- floor / heavy-duty cloths (minimum of 2)
- cotton dusters (minimum of 3)
- feather duster / synthetic fluffy duster
- long-handled brush / feather duster
- plastic bucket(s)
- plastic bowl(s)
- large pile of cloths (old tea towels, towels, t-shirts, vests, etc.)
- rubber gloves (3 pairs – 1 pair for the kitchen, 1 pair for the bathroom, 1 pair for the loo)

10 Extra Tools

These everyday items often do the job better than any sophisticated specially designed gadgets or gizmos.

old toothbrushes are great for scrubbing round taps

artists' paintbrushes are perfect for cleaning fluff from keyboards and other delicate dusting jobs

long-handled washing-up brushes can reach parts other, bigger implements can't — and they're better than cloths or sponges if you have long nails! There are numerous uses for **nail brushes**, including scrubbing showerheads and tile grout

cotton wool is suitably absorbent for tasks such as stain and limescale removal

use **small metal scrapers** for scraping off
dried food, spots of paint or greasy deposits

cotton buds soaked in water or something
stronger can be poked into all sorts of places

cocktail sticks are good for winkling
dirt out of corners, ridges and holes

wire coat hangers can be
unwound and used to probe
inaccessible places and, in an
emergency, to unblock the loo

Tools of the Trade

The Brush Off

Dirt and crumbs make a place look neglected and unclean, but a quick sweep is often all that's needed.

broom
Soft bristled is best for sweeping up fine dust and hairs and getting into corners and along skirtings.

dustpan and brush
Used in conjunction with a broom or on its own for a quick sweep up. Most are plastic but it is possible to buy old-fashioned metal dustpans, which look great but can scratch the floor. A long-handled dustpan and brush cuts out the need for a broom and for bending down.

short-handled brush
Useful for brushing off dust and debris and raising the pile on rugs and carpets (especially stairs), and for getting into, underneath and around awkward spaces and objects. The brush that comes with the dustpan is fine but you may want an extra one that is clean enough for use on fabrics and carpets.

brush care

To prolong the life and efficiency of your brooms, brushes and dustpans wash them regularly in warm soapy water. Rinse well and allow to dry thoroughly before use.

Tools of the Trade

If possible
leave mops outside
to dry — it will stop
them getting smelly.

40

Mopping Up

Mopping is a quick, easy and effective way to remove the dirt.

mop

Squeezy mops used to be all the rage but they are no good for corners so the **old-fashioned mop**, recently re-invented made out of strips of cloth, is back in favour. The new versions are light and easy to use but it is still possible to get the old string mops, which soak up a satisfying amount of water and allow you to apply a bit more welly, especially if you have large areas to clean. Replace mopheads when they get thin and straggly.

bucket

Plastic buckets with a place to squeeze the mop are essential. If you want to play at being a janitor you can opt for the galvanised bucket and stringy mop but beware — the bucket is heavy and clattery and can scratch sensitive floors.

Look out for the **double bucket** with one side for soapy water and the other for clean water for rinsing.

The Importance of a Good Cloth

You will make a better job of cleaning if you have a good cloth. Those throw-away cloths somehow just don't do the business, they leave too much wet behind and are not man enough for tough jobs. What's more they are expensive and not very eco-friendly. Invest in proper, grown-up cloths; natural fibres are best, they are more absorbent and can be wrung out more thoroughly. Cotton and linen have a texture that gives a bit of friction, essential for a good rub down.

Be thrifty and eco-minded and re-cycle old towels, tea towels, sheets, pillowcases, vests, t-shirts and old joggers, giving them a new purposeful life as dusters, polishers, dishcloths, floor cloths, window cleaners and general wipers down and moppers up.

If you don't have too many old cloths look on market stalls where you can buy towels and dishcloths at very low prices.

clean cloths

Cloth hygiene is very important as dirty and wet cloths are the perfect breeding ground for bacteria. Kill the bacteria by **soaking** cloths **regularly** in a solution of bleach. Rinse out cloths after use in cold water — bugs absolutely love warm cloths, but won't hang around to breed in cold conditions.

44

Division of Labour

It may seem obvious but don't forget to segregate your cleaning cloths and sponges, after all you wouldn't wash your face in the sink using a dish-cloth and would hopefully think twice before cleaning the loo with a face flannel.

kitchen
- **washing-up** – sponges, brushes and cloths
- **sinks and worktops** – cloth or sponge-scourer
- **floor** – even if you normally mop the floor keep a floor-cloth handy for spills and splashes
- **tea towels** – strictly for dishes, pots and pans
- **hand towel** – best to keep a separate towel for drying your hands

bathroom
- **bath, shower and basin** – sponge-scourers, brushes, cloths
- **loo** – cloth for washing and wiping down the seat and outside of the loo, loo-brush for the inside

The Score on Scourers

Careless scrubbing can cause damage so choose your scourer with care.

- **plastic knitted** – gentle yet efficient especially when used with a cream cleanser
- **steel knitted** – only to be used on tough dirt on tough objects
- **soap-impregnated wire wool** – a bit messy and can scratch, but very good for removing burned-on food from ovenware and pans
- **nylon flat** – normally green and very good for all sorts of uses from tough washing-up jobs to washing down paintwork
- **sponge / scourer** – very useful all rounder with a soft side and a tough side. Uses include washing-up, baths and decorating preparation. The standard scourer is quite abrasive but there is also a gentler version for 'non-stick' that is not so scratchy

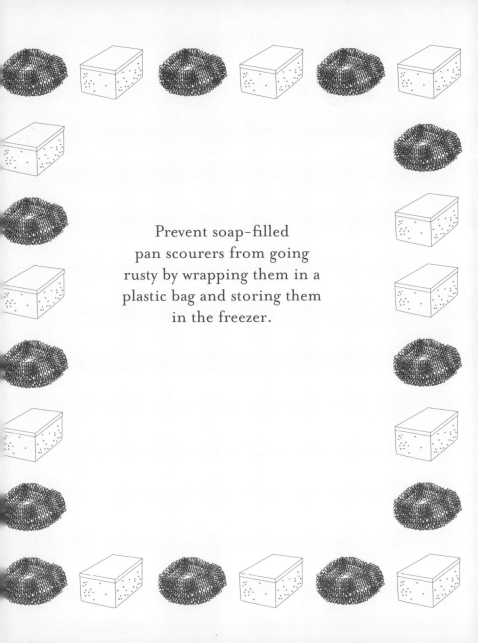

Prevent soap-filled
pan scourers from going
rusty by wrapping them in a
plastic bag and storing them
in the freezer.

The Art of Dusting

The battle against dust can never be won as it is in the air at all times, but that is no excuse to give up. The knowledge that household dust consists mostly of flakes of dead skin, moulds, insect parts and egg cases, hairs and flakes of cat saliva can turn even the most resolute slob into a devoted duster. Take as much pride in your cloths drawer as your knicker drawer: keep it well stocked and frequently laundered.

Dust duty

• Arm yourself with clean cotton dusters and a feather duster for the less accessible areas or delicate objects.

• Start at the top and work down so that dislodged dust and dirt falls down onto un-dusted areas.

• Use the duster lightly as dust contains particles that can scratch and damage surfaces if you rub too hard.

• Shake out dusters frequently otherwise you are just moving the dust around rather than getting rid of it.

• To prevent dust flying around and settling back on the things you've just dusted, slightly dampen the duster with water.

• Have a slightly damp cloth handy for removing surface dirt and marks, such as rings from cups and glasses.

• Use a vacuum cleaner or hand-held dustbuster for corners and upholstery.

• Finish the dusting programme with a thorough vacuuming.

50

Damp Dusting

A damp duster will pick up more dust than a dry one, as well as prevent it from flying around. However, it shouldn't be too damp. Using a spray bottle filled with water (add a few drops of lemon oil or lavender for a nice smell and more effective cleaning) will achieve the right level of dampness.

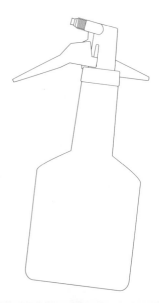

Feather Pleasure

• If dusting doesn't tickle your fancy, try a feather duster. More fun than a boring cloth, it allows you to dust round things without moving them.

• Perfect for dusting high shelves it may also inspire you to dust ledges, light-fittings, lampshades, pictures and precious ornaments and even flick the dust off the tops of books. A long-handled feather duster allows you to get to cobwebs on the ceiling and into all sorts of awkward spaces.

• Splash out on a good-quality feather duster as the cheap ones can be scratchy and leave feathery bits in their wake.

• The synthetic, fluffy dusters are also good, but they don't get into the places other feathers reach, are generally heavier and therefore less sensitive to nooks and crannies and, if you're not careful, more prone to knocking things over.

• Shake out feather and synthetic dusters frequently as you dust.

• Wash synthetic dusters in soapy water, rinse well but do not use softeners as this reduces static, which is what picks up the dust.

Tools of the Trade

53

3 Clean Machines

You will make a more thorough job of cleaning with a little help from your friends the vacuum cleaner and its little helper the dustbuster.

Vacuum Cleaners

Essential for sucking dirt, dust and nasties out of your carpet, vacuum cleaners are also great for bare floors, upholstery, beds, curtains and general dusting. When choosing your machine, you need to consider:

style

Choose a model that can be stored in an accessible space — you will be more likely to use it if you can get at it easily. Cylinder types are the most popular and versatile. An upright cleaner may be easier on acres of carpet but isn't easy to carry upstairs. If you opt for this type make sure it has a hose and long-handled attachment for stairs, corners and edges.

tools

The tools are very important so look before you buy. Ideally they will include a narrow nozzle, dusting brush, upholstery nozzle, general purpose brush attachment and a floor brush with bristles that won't scratch those fashionably bare floors.

power

Believe it or not, vacuum cleaners can be too powerful. Some of the super models will suck the fibres right out of your expensive carpet and the feathers out of your cushions – you have been warned! Traditional vacuum cleaners lose suction power as the bag or chamber fills up, unlike the cyclone vacuum cleaners, which work by centrifugal force and do not lose suction. Variable suction settings is a useful feature especially for more delicate items such as curtains.

dust disposal

With a bagless vacuum cleaner dust is collected in the body of the machine and is easy to empty (and the see-through dirt chamber provides an entertaining, if sobering, view of what has been lurking in your home). Replaceable bags are also easy to dispose of but can be expensive, and wasteful, though you can re-use the bag.

10 Uses for a Vacuum Cleaner

carpets and rugs

beds

curtains

slatted blinds

bare floors

upholstery

general dusting

high up cobwebs

tops of door and
window frames,
wardrobes and
other high surfaces

DIY preparation
and cleaning up

Dust Busters

Dustbusters are small hand-held,
wire-free, battery-run vacuum cleaners,
which are charged up by plugging into
a normal electric socket.

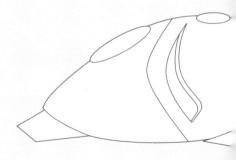

10 things dustbusters are useful for:

- quick tidy-ups for unexpected visitors
- dealing with accidental spills such as the contents of a badly opened cereal packet
- getting into awkward corners, under and behind things
- persuading teenagers to do their bit
- picking up crumbs and bits from inside cupboards
- picking up the dust from small DIY jobs such as drilling holes
- cleaning out bags, baskets and suitcases
- getting rid of hairs and other bits of dirt from pets' beds
- picking up hairs and fluff from clothing
- cleaning inside cars

Clean Machines

61

4 Beasts, Bugs and Bacteria

We are surrounded by millions of microbes. Most are harmless, some can make us sick and a few, such as Salmonella, can make us very ill indeed. Infections are mostly associated with food hygiene so it's worth developing good habits in the kitchen. But don't go mad, exposure to bacteria and viruses helps build up immunity, so insisting on a sterile environment in your own home makes you vulnerable to otherwise mild bugs you may pick up outside.

Allergy Alert

Allergies are an adverse reaction to allergens. While some reactions can be dangerous, others are mild. An adverse reaction may be a 'sensitivity' rather than a full-blown 'allergy'. A number of allergens are present in air and household dust, including VOCs (volatile organic compounds) that are vapours released from chemicals found in household cleaners, air fresheners, paints and stain removers.

action

- Keep the dust down with regular dusting and vacuuming
- Launder bedlinen, clothes and textiles frequently
- Keep dust-gathering clutter to a minimum
- Avoid 'super' cleaning products that contain harsh chemicals
- Maintain good ventilation

common reactions

headaches

skin rashes

breathing problems, including asthma

nausea

dizziness

sore throat

itchy nose

common allergens

fungal spores

faeces, egg cases and dead bits of insects

hairs and faeces of rodents

chemicals used in cleaning products, air-fresheners
and paints

common sources

damp

mould

dust mites

cockroaches

cats, dogs and birds

Beasts, Bugs and Bacteria

Unwelcome Visitors

We share our homes with a vast number of living creatures, while most are harmless, some are a potential health threat. Grubby surfaces, open packets of food, crumbs, last night's leftovers and unwashed dishes provide a running buffet for many of these hungry creatures.

Flies bring in and spread bacteria. They not only eat your food but lay eggs on it, which soon hatch out into maggots, which grow into more flies.

Cockroaches can carry dangerous diseases such as dysentery, gastroenteritis and typhoid and as well as food they also enjoy hair, leather, wallpaper and faeces.

Fleas prefer pets, but they sometimes bite humans. Their eggs – often laid in carpets – can lay dormant for years until a suitable tasty doggy or moggy comes along.

Moths lay their eggs on your best clothes, linens and carpets, which become food for the hatched maggots.

Mosquitos spread malaria, but not all of them do. However, the bites itch like mad.

Mice spread germs and droppings, and the fact that they wee as they run along is enough to put anyone off.

Rats carry Weils disease — a nasty and potentially fatal illness caught by contact with their urine. No-one in their right mind wants rats in their home.

There are plenty of effective insecticides and poisons on the market, but many are toxic and therefore dangerous, especially if you have pets and young children. They can also provoke allergic reactions. If you have a real 'infestation' of insects or vermin, you are advised to call in the professionals, otherwise, try these more friendly deterrents.

Insects don't like strong smells so burning eucalyptus, lavender, citronella, wintergreen or peppermint on an oil burner will keep them away. **Mosquitos** in particular dislike citronella. **Moths** will leave your linens alone if you store them with cottonwool balls dipped in lavender, eucalyptus or rosemary oil.

Scented plants also help, try basil and verbena for **flies** while mint will deter **ants**.

If the **ants** persist try sprinkling red pepper or chilli powder at their point of entry.

Trapping is okay for one or two troublesome **mice** (bait traps with dried fruit, not cheese). If you can't face dead bodies use a humane trap and release the miscreant back into the wild, preferably somewhere far away. If you are brave you can try to trap a **rat** (they love Brazil nuts), but rats rarely live alone so it is best to contact your local authority or a specialist company who will send in the rat-catcher.

Catching Cockroaches

You can make your own pesticide-free trap using a **jar** with a **slice of white bread** inside. A **piece of wood** such as a ruler will help them get into the jar and a coating of **petroleum jelly** on the inside of the jar mouth will cause the cockroaches to fall in and also stop them from escaping. They can be killed with hot soapy water or by placing them in the freezer overnight. Alternatively, adding borax to the bait will kill them but don't use this if there are children or pets in the house.

Dust Mites – The Awful Truth

Too small to be seen with the naked eye, these tiny creatures thrive in warm, moist places and feast on flakes of dead skin. Unsurprisingly their ideal homes include mattresses, pillows and bedding, but they are happy to take up residence in carpets, cushions, upholstered furniture and cuddly toys. They don't spread disease but the dust from their dead bodies and egg cases are the allergens that can provoke allergies in humans, especially asthmatics.

5 ways to fight the mite

1 Wash bedlinen at minimum 60°C.
2 Avoid padded headboards. Go for a wooden or metal–framed bed with open slats rather than a divan.
3 Clutter attracts dust, so keep it under control.
4 Mites can be killed by freezing so put duvets, pillows and soft toys into a chest freezer for at least six hours every six months or so – or more if they are a big problem. This kills the mites, but not the allergens which will have to be removed by washing.
5 Avoid fitted carpets and curtains and opt instead for bare floors, washable rugs and blinds.

Beasts, Bugs and Bacteria

Now Wash Your Hands... Properly!

Amazingly, people are getting very lazy about washing their hands. Some don't bother while others make do with a quick, ineffective rinse and a wipe on a microbe-laden towel. Make sure you give your hands a proper wash before and after handling food. You know it makes sense.

1 Wet your hands.
2 Soap thoroughly and rub your hands together, making sure you get in between the fingers – and don't forget the backs of your hands and wrists.
3 Scrub your nails if you have been handling raw meat, tackling a very dirty job or digging the garden.
4 Rinse the soap (you don't want to leave it covered in bacteria).
5 Rinse your hands thoroughly under clean, running water.
6 Dry thoroughly on a clean towel rubbing briskly to remove any remaining microbes. Wet hands spread germs much more effectively than dry.

Don't forget to change hand towels frequently as they often harbour bugs and bacteria passed from less well-washed hands and less scrupulous users.

Food Watch

If you've ever had food poisoning, you are unlikely to want to repeat the experience. As most cases are caused by infections picked up in the home, it is worth taking a few precautions in food areas even if the rest of your home is less than pristine.

keep clean
Make sure there is no food left around in any form, including crumbs and smears. Wash your hands before and after handling food and in between different foodstuffs, such as meat or fish.

keep dry
Bugs dislike dry surfaces and atmospheres so keep everywhere well ventilated and keep foodstuffs in airtight containers. Don't keep food in packets if your cupboards are damp.

keep cool

Run fridges and freezers at the correct temperature — a maximum of 4°C for a fridge, -18°C for a freezer — and, if possible, store other foodstuffs in cool places.

keep tidy

More clutter provides more opportunities and more surfaces for dust and dirt to settle and for insects and bacteria to accumulate and breed.

food bug danger zones:

hands
sinks and bowls
dishcloths
work surfaces
chopping boards
rubbish bins

5 Bacteria Killers

Chlorine bleach is effective on most household germs and is useful for wiping down work surfaces and soaking cloths and items such as hairbrushes and even children's toys. Use neat for pouring down loos, sinks and drains but always dilute it with water for other general uses.

• Wiping down worktops and surfaces:
60ml to 5 litres water
• Soaking fabrics, cloths, toys, hairbrushes etc:
20ml to 5 litres water, leave for 45 minutes and rinse thoroughly.
• Soaking overnight: 10ml to 5 litres water, rinse well, keep a solution in a spray bottle for use on worktops and chopping boards.

Vinegar is a natural, non-toxic disinfectant. Use for wiping down work surfaces and for sinks and basins: 1 part vinegar to 1 part water.

Tea-tree oil is a natural disinfectant and deodoriser and is also effective as a fungicide. Wipe down surfaces with a solution of 2 teaspoons of tea tree oil added to 2 cups of water or put it in a spray bottle for use on mould and mildew.

Borax is a disinfectant, insecticide and deodoriser. Mixed with bicarbonate of soda it makes a good general-purpose germ-killing cleaner and can also be used for soaking fabrics.

Heat kills a lot of bacteria. Washing bedlinen, towels and cloths at 60°C helps keep the bugs at bay. Boiling is good for dishcloths and boiling water can be poured onto utensils and chopping boards or down plugholes.

Solar Power

Sunshine is the best natural disinfectant and various items in your home will benefit from a sunbathing session. The sun's heat and rays kill bacteria and creatures such as dust mites. If you have a garden, patio or balcony put them outside, if you haven't then don't be afraid to hang things out of the window, continental-style. If possible, dry your washing outdoors.

10 items to benefit from a day in the sun

- duvets and pillows
- bed covers and throws
- mattresses — futons will love it
- children's toys — especially soft ones
- cushions — the sun fluffs up the feathers
- rugs, dhurries and kelims
- anything with pet and urine stains
- fabric stains — they will fade in the sun
- clothes that get dry-cleaned rather than washed
- shoes — especially trainers, take the laces out and open them up to the sunshine

82

Spore Wars

Edible fungi are delicious but the sort of fungi that inhabit your refrigerator or grow on your walls, shower curtains and in between your toes are not so appetising. There are millions of spores, yeasts, moulds and mildew flying around your home looking for somewhere to live and breed. They are common components of house dust and can cause allergies and infections. They love damp, moist conditions so are most happy in **steamy bathrooms** and **unventilated spaces** where they make themselves visible in the form of **black spots** and splodges, which can grow at an alarming rate.

Given the chance, they **rot wood** and walls and can carry **infections**, such as ringworm and athletes foot. At the extreme end, they cause Legionnaires disease, which is a killer. Fungal spores also invade humidifiers, dehumidifiers and vaporisers and set up home in tile grout, sealants, refrigerator drip trays and food. The best defence against these invaders is to avoid damp conditions through **proper ventilation** and **good housekeeping**.

Beasts, Bugs and Bacteria

Coming Up For Air

Nowadays we tend to work and live in heated, air-conditioned, double-glazed, sealed, microclimates that create warm, moist, stuffy environments much enjoyed by bugs and bacteria. Poor ventilation can cause headaches, sore throats, allergies and unpleasant smells. One of the easiest ways to remedy this situation is to open a window.

5 reasons to throw open a window

1 **Let** out stale air, steam, exhaled breath, perspiration and cooking smells.

2 **Give** some of those flakes of skin, insect body parts and other unwholesome ingredients of dust the chance to escape.

3 **Keep** air circulating – vital for good health and preventing the build up of moisture.

4 **Avoid** a build up of VOCs (volatile organic compounds) given off from common household products, paint, adhesives and substances such as fire-retardants present in many carpets and fabrics.

5 **Replenish** the air and reduce the effects of negative ions caused by static from computers, etc.

Olfactory Outlets

WARNING!

Bad smells are caused by a variety of things including damp, mildew, rotten food, dirt and fetid footwear. Although some are short-term and unavoidable many are the result of poor hygiene and ventilation. However, we have become over-sensitive when it comes to smells; this paranoia is fed by the adverts for air 'fresheners' that keep our homes free from odours, which may suggest we are anything but clean-living, sweet-smelling, bacteria-free citizens.

No-one would deny the advantage of a quick burst of air freshener in the loo but 'deodorising' every room is not only daft but dangerous. It has recently been reported that these products cause respiratory problems, especially in babies, young children and those with asthma. Air fresheners work either by masking the smell with a strong, synthetic odour or by de-sensitising our sense of smell by coating the nasal passages with a film or blocking the olfactory nerve. De-sensitisation could be dangerous as it could render us unable to smell bad food or something burning.

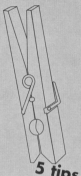

5 tips for reducing smells

1 open a window
2 install extractor fans
3 when cooking fish, place a small bowl of
white vinegar next to the stove
4 a lighted candle in the kitchen during
cooking also reduces smells
5 vanilla extract on a cottonwool ball in the
bathroom is an effective deodoriser

Beasts, Bugs and Bacteria

87

Smell As Sweet

It is easy to scent your home naturally, which is not only safer and nicer, but much cheaper too.

essential oils

A few drops of your favourite essential oil to a small amount of water in the top of an oil burner will scent a room subtly and safely. Alternatively try a dab of fragrant oil on a lightbulb.

plants and flowers

Scented plants and cut flowers are the best of natural smells but take care as some of the more highly scented can be a bit much in a small room and can cause an allergic reaction. Place scented plants near to windows and doors.

herbs and spices

• Sprinkle cinnamon, nutmeg and cloves in a small pan of water and simmer.

• Put lavender or herbs in the bag or cylinder of your vacuum cleaner.

• Put a good handful of crushed, dried herbs such as rosemary or lavender in a jar with 2 tablespoons bicarbonate of soda, shake well, sprinkle on to carpets and rugs. Leave for an hour before vacuuming up.

Beasts, Bugs and Bacteria

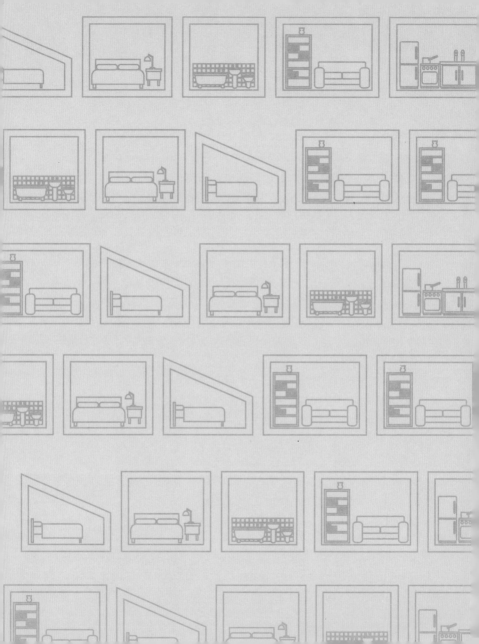

5 Order of Service

For many of us the words 'routine' and 'order' are a turn-off, but when it comes to cleaning a little of both can save time and effort and bring harmony to the home.

Living Areas

beauty routine
Regular cleansing keeps your home looking good
and makes you feel better.

freshen-up (daily)
• open windows
• take out dirty cups, last night's pizza and any
clothes (especially trainers and socks)
• plump up cushions
• remove any bits, spills or nasties on the floor with
a dustbuster or damp cloth

cleanse (weekly)
• open windows
• dust all surfaces
• vacuum all flooring and mop bare floors
• remove old newspapers and magazines

deep cleanse (monthly)

• shake and plump up cushions first — if you do it later you will add dust to already dusted areas

• dust all surfaces plus the individual objects on them — there is no need to clear bookshelves but dust the shelves and the tops of the books

• don't forget ledges, the tops of pictures, the legs of chairs, tables and other furniture

• dust slatted blinds using a duster, special gadget or vacuum cleaner attachment

• take off seat cushions and using the appropriate attachments vacuum upholstery, heavy curtains and roller blinds

• vacuum floors using attachments for edges, corners, tops of skirting boards, and underneath furniture. If you are very houseproud you will move sofas and chairs in order to clean the floor underneath

• mop bare floors using appropriate methods (see floor care)

Bedroom Routines

freshen-up (daily)
• open windows — even ten minutes is helpful
• pull the bedclothes back to allow the bed to air
• plump up the pillows
• put dirty clothes in the linen basket
• put clothing to be worn again on a chair to allow it to air
• remove any mugs, tumblers, plates or old food

cleanse (weekly or fortnightly depending on your standards)
• remove pillow cases, duvet cover and bottom sheet
• turn the mattress over (especially if it is a futon)
• sort out clothes and put dirty clothes and bed-linen in the linen basket
• return clothes, shoes and accessories to their rightful places
• dust all surfaces, starting at the highest points and working down
• use a damp cloth to wipe up stains such as spilled make-up

- remove any rubbish such as used tissues and cotton wool
- re-make the bed with clean bed-linen
- vacuum floor, mop any bare floors

deep cleanse

- vacuum under the bed
- vacuum the mattress every six months or so

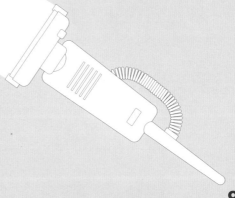

Bedtime Stories

• On average, we spend approximately a third of our lives in bed.

• During sleep our body loses around a cup of water from perspiration which ends up in our sheets, blankets and the mattress.

• Because we spend so long in bed, the quality of air in the bedroom is more important than in any other room.

• Most asthma attacks happen at night probably triggered by several hours of exposure to dust, poor ventilation and air-borne microbes and allergens.

• The less cluttered and messy your bedroom the better you sleep.

• Every time you turn over you shed hundreds of flakes of dead skin — heaven for dust mites.

• While sleeping even the cleanest most perfumed people exude skin oils and body smells, breathe out moisture, breath smells and microorganisms into the air, pillow and bedding. Two in a bed doubles the amounts.

Kitchen Drill

✔ daily

• put away all foodstuffs, and if they are kept on open shelves, make sure they are in airtight, bacteria-proof containers
• wash dishes
• wipe down work surfaces and remove spills and splodges

✔ weekly

• clean all work surfaces and underneath appliances, such as kettles, toasters and any other items stored on worktops
• clean the cooker hob
• throw out old and bad food — make sure nothing nasty is lurking at the back of the fridge
• wipe down the outside of the fridge
• clean the floor
• empty the bins and rinse out

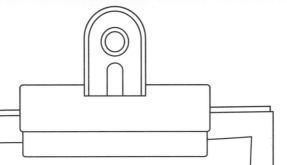

✔ **1–3 monthly** (depending on your dirt-tolerance level)
• wipe down the inside of the fridge, wipe or rinse shelves and wash out fruit and veg storage drawers
• scrub down the worktops
• clean the hob and oven
• wipe around door and drawer handles
• de-frost the freezer
• mop or scrub the floor thoroughly making an effort to get into corners and underneath things

Bathroom Routine

cleanse (daily)
• hang up all towels and bath mats to allow the air to circulate and dry them
• mop up any obvious puddles
• rinse any scum from the basin and bath – use a sponge, cloth or quick blast of spray cleaner
• leave the shower curtain in a closed position to dry and prevent the growth of smelly mould

deep cleanse (weekly – no excuses, if you don't do this weekly you are a slob)
• put all used towels and mats into the wash
• clear any surfaces ready for cleaning
• empty the bin and throw away any rubbish
• clean the loo
• clean the bath, shower and basin
• wipe over all surfaces, including tiles and mirrors (a spray cleaner is quick and easy)
• vacuum the floor first to get up any dust and bits then mop or, as bathroom floors are usually quite small, get on your hands and knees to give it the works
• put out fresh towels and bath mats

When running a bath, put the cold water in first as this reduces the amount of steam produced

6 Clean and Tidy

With copious quantities of dirt and dust swirling around the atmosphere waiting to settle on any available surface it makes sense to provide the minimum opportunity for it to do so. Good storage is the key.

Kitchen Tidy

Keep surfaces
as clear as
possible to
allow for easy,
and thorough,
cleaning.

5 ways to keep things out of the way

1 Cupboards and drawers. Protect objects from dust and grease.

2 Open shelves look nice, provide an opportunity for display and keep things off work surfaces and tabletops.

3 Even if you are not a keen cook a 'batterie de cuisine' of pots, pans and utensils hanging in your kitchen will look impressive whether it is a purpose-made fitment or a simple pole hung with butchers' hooks.

4 Store unruly foodstuffs in tins, jars and other airtight containers (but keep the labels for reference, ie. instructions, sell-by dates).
Tuck them away in a cupboard or admire them on open shelves.

5 A rubbish bin fixed to the inside of a cupboard door or in a purpose-built unit leaves the floor clear and easier to clean.

Clean and Tidy

Tidy Your Bedroom

Your mother wasn't just nagging when she told you to tidy your bedroom. Leaving clothes and bits of cotton wool, tissues, mugs and plates lying around is bad for the clothes, bad for hygiene and bad for your image... so get tidying.

Keeping your best clothes under wraps is a good idea but always use breathable plastic or fabric covers.

Air circulation in a wardrobe will deter moths, mites and mildew and help prevent that fusty, charity shop smell developing. If your wardrobe is airless open the door occasionally.

Now you know all about perspiration, shedding skin and those dust mites you may want to think twice before putting today's jumper (slightly damp and with a fresh supply of skin scales) back in the drawer with the clean stuff. Allow them to air by hanging them up on a hook or placing them over the back of a chair or loosely folded on the seat.

A hanging rail, whether as a cheap alternative to a wardrobe or a solution for overspill, is a good idea but keep clothes dust-free by covering with a sheet or something jolly or pretty.

It is sensible to utilise space under the bed for extra storage but don't just shove everything out of sight. Keep things in boxes, baskets or purpose-made under-bed storage, some of which have castors for ease of access to the contents and for cleaning.

You know it makes
sense to lock away
all drugs to prevent
them getting into
the wrong hands
— and mouths.

Bathroom Storage

cabinet secrets

Keeping a bathroom clean requires quite a bit of effort, but it is a lot easier if you avoid cluttering up shelves, windowsills and surfaces with all those lotions and potions essential for keeping you clean and beautiful. Clusters of bottles, boxes, sprays, plastic containers and dispensers are rarely attractive – and some products are best kept private – so keep them out of sight in a good-looking cupboard or cabinet, which will not only make your bathroom look better but will be easier to keep clean.

play and display

As any interiors magazine will tell you, pretty bottles, piles of towels, flannels, sponges and soaps transform your bathroom into something special. However, display can easily turn into clutter, which makes cleaning a difficult and tedious exercise. Displaying such things in attractive bowls, baskets and other containers will make cleaning easier. But don't forget to clean those out occasionally as well!

Clean Living

It is easier to keep the living room clean (and tidy) if you:

keep stuff to a minimum

You don't have to be a minimalist but control the spread of cushions, objects and unnecessary pieces of furniture.

keep stuff off the floor

If you provide a shelf, surface or storage for anything and everything from magazines to cups of coffee you are less likely to suffer from shrinking floorspace.

think big

Fiddly storage 'solutions' are often shunned by those not devoted to interior design, but even reluctant slobs might be tempted to put newspapers, CDs or toys into large containers, such as baskets and boxes. These also make a quick tidy-up a lot easier.

litter bug

Provide a rubbish bin - you never know it might get used.

keep behind closed doors

Open shelves may be one of the great storage successes of recent times but can descend into messy chaos in the wrong hands. Cupboards rather than open shelves create an aura of calm even if chaos lurks behind the door. If you want to keep control but still have things on display, go for glass-fronted cupboards and cabinets.

File Away

If you don't enjoy cleaning at the best of times it's even more daunting when your home appears to have been invaded by the paper monster who has deposited piles of paperwork, junk mail, newspapers and magazines on every available surface. Dealing with paper piles need not be too painful if you set up a simple, uncomplicated filing system. Get rid of the piles and the dust and detritus will have fewer places to hide.

Stage 1   **Save** or **Dump** (weekly or fortnightly)
Stage 2   Recyle all the **Dump** and then divide the **Save** into **Do Now** and **Do Later** (weekly or fortnightly)
Stage 3   File all the **Do Later** (whenever you have the time or the inclination)

basic equipment

To make filing easy and encourage others to join in, equip yourself with storage that looks nice on its own, is big enough and preferably doesn't have a lid — the removal of which might be too much for some to cope with. Suggestions are:

• **baskets** — an attractive asset to any home and available in a wide variety of shapes and sizes.
• **cardboard magazine holders** — perfect for magazines but also good for archiving any paperwork. Why not have several of these holders and skip straight to Stage 3?
• **bulldog clips** — great for keeping papers under control and for filing by subject. Look for big fat clips in bright colours. Can be hung on hooks.

What's the Hook?

Putting things away takes time and commitment and for many it is something they are totally disinclined to do. If opening drawers and cupboards is a daunting prospect, try a hook, probably the simplest form of storage. To encourage children (and childish adults) invest in novelty hooks, there are plenty around with pictures on or made in the shape of animals.

get hooked

- **hallway** – coats, bags, baskets, shoes, keys, umbrellas, sports equipment
- **kitchen** – dishcloths, rubber gloves, tea towels, towels, aprons
- **bathroom** – towels, face flannels, mats, laundry bags, make-up bags
- **bedroom** – clothes, accessories, laundry bags, jewellery, scarves
- **backs of doors** – clothes, laundry bags, shoe-storage
- **anywhere** – bulldog-clipped bills, correspondence, lists, recipes and anything else you need easy access to

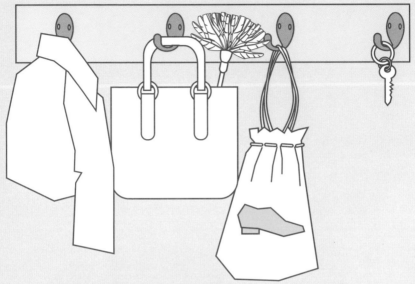

Don't waste the storage opportunities of
hung-up bags and baskets, which can be
filled with everything from shoes, gloves
and scarves to dusters and general junk.

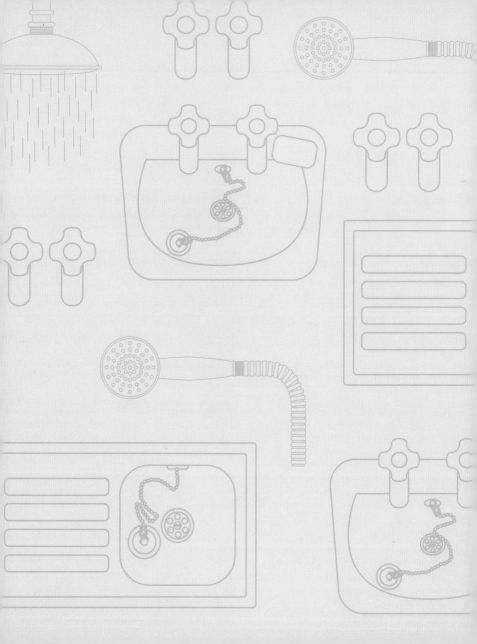

7 Water Features

Even if you neglect the rest of your home, wherever water is involved deserves special attention as these are the places where hygiene is likely to be an issue. Be aware that stains can also be a stain on your character and that dirty sinks, baths, showers and loos can provoke a number of reactions from mild disgust to outright condemnation.

Limescale

what is it?

Limescale is formed from the deposits in 'hard' water, which is high in dissolved minerals, mostly calcium and magnesium.

what does it do?

Though it is not a health risk it causes a hard, beige-brown build-up on and around taps, shower fittings, sinks and inside kettles. Not only is it unsightly, it affects performance. It clogs up the little holes in shower fittings reducing power, and a build-up in kettles, washing and dishwashing machines as well as heating systems affects efficiency and energy use. If you have a big problem you could look at getting a water-softening system installed, or use water-softening agents in washing machines and dishwashers.

Although it is an effective limescale remover, vinegar is an acid that, if used too strong and for too long, will eat into the surface of an enamelled bath, dulling its appearance and making it less dirt-resistant.

limescale removal

As limescale consists mostly of calcium, which is an alkali, it needs an acid to dissolve it. There are several efficient, de-scaling products on the market but vinegar is a simpler and cheaper alternative. A wipe or scrub with a cloth dipped in neat vinegar will remove light deposits but the harder stuff requires more effort.

Remove showerheads and soak in a solution of 1 part water to 1 part vinegar. Scrub off any remaining deposits using a nail- or toothbrush and, if necessary, use a needle or pin to poke it out from the holes.

To remove limescale from taps fill a plastic bag with cotton wool soaked in a generous amount of vinegar. Place the bag over the tap making sure the vinegary cotton wool is in close contact with the affected parts, and put an elastic band round the neck of the bag to prevent the vinegar seeping out.

Keep on top of the limescale by spraying sinks, showers and baths regularly with a weak vinegar solution, leave for a few minutes before rinsing off.

Water Features

121

Dirty Scum

what is it?

Soaps and detergents combine with the mineral salts in water to form the scum, which gets left behind on sinks, baths, basins, shower trays and tiles. It builds up over time to form a dull, greyish film. Along with the scum there is bound to be a certain amount of dirt and grease from the washing of bodies and dishes, all of which is attractive to bacteria, mould and mildew and unattractive to fellow washers and bathers.

preventative measures

As with all dirt a quick spray with good-old vinegar and water solution or proprietary spray cleaner after bathing or showering will keep the scum away.

If you can't be bothered to spritz after each bath or shower, use a cream or general-purpose cleanser at least once a week. Rinse well and wipe over with a dry cloth or towel.

big scum

If no-one has done either of the above or you have just moved into a new property previously inhabited by scummy people, you have to make more effort. This mostly means using a scourer and extra cleaning material – a mildly abrasive cream cleanser is good though a spray cleanser is easier to apply – buy one specially formulated for getting rid of soap scum. As soap scum is mostly alkali and body dirt is mostly acidic you need a two-pronged attack using both vinegar and bicarbonate of soda or their commercial equivalents.

Using a foam bath reduces the amount of scum left behind.

Mildew

what is it?

When some of those millions of fungal spores flying around us find a nice, damp, warm place to live they breed and form ever-expanding unsightly, black growths which give off a fusty, musty smell. Danger zones are tiles — especially the grouting and sealants round sinks, baths, basins and showers.

prevention

Keep the atmosphere as dry as possible with good ventilation and frequent wiping down of wet surfaces. If you have a severe moisture problem, install a fan.

cure

Specialist mildew treatments are available that are efficient and easy to use, but good results can be achieved with homemade alternatives.

For **general staining** spray with bleach solution (150ml household bleach in 1.5 litres water) leave for half an hour, scrub and rinse.

For **tougher, blacker stains** make a paste with borax and lemon juice or vinegar — leave on for half an hour and scrub off.

To remove mildew from **tile grout** mix 2 parts baking soda, 1 part borax and enough hot water to make a thick paste, apply to grout and scrub with a soft brush — rinse well.

To remove mould from **sealant** round the bath, basins and shower trays wipe with neat vinegar then wipe with a paste of bicarbonate of soda.

In Sink

A dirty sink is not only a health hazard it says something about its owner.

cleaning

Use a good squeeze of multi-purpose liquid or cream cleanser or, if you are into alternatives, a paste of baking powder and water. A sponge scourer (the softer, 'non-stick' variety) is best as it can be flipped over to scrub heavier dirt.

stains

Water spots and rust marks can usually be removed with a little extra cleanser and a bit more effort but if they refuse to budge try giving them a good rub with a soft cloth dipped in neat vinegar.

exceptions and observations

Stainless steel is the most common material and is very robust, hygienic and easy to clean. But don't expect new sinks to retain that brilliant shine; accept that they will develop a more muted, matt glow.

Enamelled sinks scratch easily and also chip, so be careful with those heavy pans. Avoid harsh abrasives and scourers and acid-based cleaning products.

Porcelain sinks are unforgiving if you drop anything so be careful. They develop a crazed surface over time which can lead to staining. To freshen them up and remove stains fill with a water and bleach solution and leave for half an hour.

Acrylic sinks should be treated more gently. Don't use harsh abrasives or scourers. Follow any manufacturer's instructions.

Composite materials can be cleaned using mild cream cleanser and a soft scourer. For stains follow the manufacturer's instructions, which may advise the use of a fine abrasive paper.

Water Features

Kitchen Sink Drama

Allowing tea leaves, coffee grounds and bits of food to go down the plughole is asking for trouble. Blockages are not pleasant and bad ones can require drastic action. Stop stuff going down the plug by covering the plughole with a sink strainer and get into the habit of pouring boiling water down the plug-hole occasionally to melt grease and goo.

If the waste does get blocked there are various forms of action.

Try an old-fashioned sink plunger. Make sure you have an air-tight seal around the plughole – and if you have a double sink make sure the other plughole is plugged. Press up and down vigorously and see what happens.

Pour about 100g bicarbonate of soda down the plughole followed by 250ml vinegar poured very slowly. This should create a satisfying fizz which, hopefully, will clear the blockage.

If you have any of those big fizzy indigestion relief tablets in the medicine cabinet, pop two down the plughole followed by 250ml vinegar.

Tip 100g salt and 100g baking powder down followed by a kettleful of boiling water.

Pour down 2 tablespoons washing soda dissolved in 1 litre hot water.

If none of the above work try one of the many proprietary products which usually come in powder form. They can be expensive but are usually effective and therefore worth it but follow the instructions carefully as they contain harsh and toxic chemicals.

The Art of Washing Up

Equipment...

plastic washing-up bowl (optional) *
sponge scourer,

washing-up brush (with nice long handle),
bottle brush, dish cloth

* If you have a double sink it is best to wash up
directly in the sink, but if not a bowl is useful as
you can chuck stuff down the sink while you are
washing up. A bowl also provides a softer surface
for sensitive dishes.

How to Wash Up

1 **Scrape** off food scraps.

2 **Rinse** to remove excess goo (optional, but you won't have to change the washing-up water as often).

3 **Stack** scraped and rinsed dishes, cups, mugs and glasses in orderly piles.

4 **Fill** a sink or bowl with hot water and a good squeeze of washing-up liquid.

5 **Wash** glasses first followed by the least dirty items and ending with the tough stuff. Use a scourer on bits of dried-on food and a washing-up brush on the insides of mugs and in between the prongs of forks.

6 **Change** the water as soon as it looks murky.

7 **Rinse** to remove suds, which leave residues that some people prefer not to ingest. Running water is best but a more eco-friendly alternative is to dunk them in the second sink or bowl of clean hot water.

8 **Drain** in a dish drainer making sure any mugs, cups, bowls and pans are upside down.

9 **Dry** either by leaving to drain or with a clean tea towel. Have a generous stack of tea towels to hand so that you don't wipe things with a wet, grubby one.

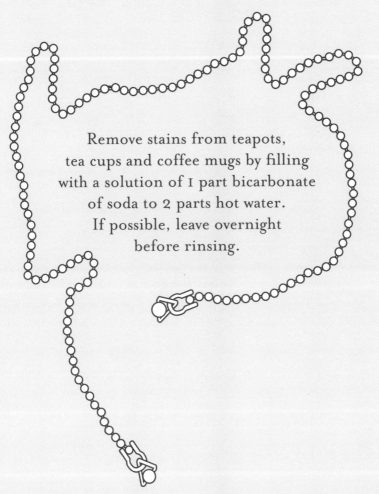

Remove stains from teapots,
tea cups and coffee mugs by filling
with a solution of 1 part bicarbonate
of soda to 2 parts hot water.
If possible, leave overnight
before rinsing.

Pots and Pans

Cooking is pleasurable but washing-up is not so much fun. The job is less of a chore if you always fill pots, pans and ovenware with water and a squeeze of washing-up liquid as soon as you have finished using them. If you do this most food deposits will come off easily with the help of a scourer, if necessary.

- For **burnt-on food** fill the ovenware with hot water, add 1 tablespoon bicarbonate of soda and soak.
- Remove **burned-on stains** on old ovenproof glassware with a soap-filled pad.
- Never use abrasives on **non-stick pans**, use a plastic scourer and a small amount of washing-up liquid.
- To prevent **untreated cast iron** from going rusty wash by hand, dry thoroughly then brush the inside with a thin layer of vegetable oil.
- Soak **enamelled pots** in hot soapy water. Never fill a hot pan with cold water; make sure the pan has cooled before washing, rinsing and drying. Remove stubborn residues with a plastic or sponge scourer. Pans with metal or plastic handles can be washed in a dishwasher but those with wooden handles should be washed by hand.
- Clean **aluminium pans** with a solution of 115ml vinegar to 1 litre water (neat vinegar eats into aluminium). Boil and then simmer for 10 minutes.
- **Stainless steel pans** develop a rainbow effect after a while. The insides can be cleaned as for aluminium or use a proprietary stainless steel cleaner.

Baths and Basins

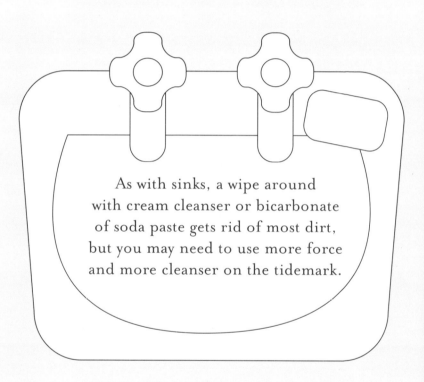

As with sinks, a wipe around with cream cleanser or bicarbonate of soda paste gets rid of most dirt, but you may need to use more force and more cleanser on the tidemark.

- Avoid acidic cleaners on **enamel baths and sinks** as they erode the surface. A **plastic scourer** is a good non-scratch cleaning implement. Use **white spirit** for stains.
- It is easier to clean the **bath** when it is **warm**, so tackle it straight after getting out.
- Keep a spray bottle of **vinegar solution** or **proprietary cleaner** handy to spritz baths and basins immediately after use, leaving for a few minutes before rinsing off.
- A **magnetic holder** keeps **soap** dry (and hygienic) and prevents soggy soap scum clogging up the basin.
- Give **taps** a quick polish with a little **toothpaste** (not the gel sort). Rub it on with your finger, rinse and polish with a dry cloth.
- Never use scourers or abrasives on **acrylic** baths, neat **washing-up liquid** on a soft cloth is a neat idea, as is **liquid laundry detergent** for tidemarks.
- Keep cleaning materials **handy** to encourage you (and others) to use them.

Refreshing Showers

After a shower, the last thing you want (or have time) to do is clean up after you. It is the polite thing to do, however, especially if you share the bathroom with others, but even if you don't, it will be more pleasant to use the next time.

The après shower habit

1 Rinse the shower tray and tiles using the showerhead.

2 Spray the tiles with vinegar solution in a spray bottle or scrape any excess water and soap off the tiles using a shower squeegee (available from catalogues and shops).

3 Pull the shower curtain across to allow it to dry or wipe down the glass screen with a dry towel or cloth dedicated to that purpose.

• To remove mildew from machine-washable **shower curtains** wash in the washing machine with laundry detergent and, if possible, several old towels which will act as scourers. Use a warm wash cycle and put 1 cup of white vinegar in the final rinse to deter regrowth. For non-machine-washable curtains try scrubbing with a paste of bicarbonate of soda or leaving to soak overnight in a mild bleach solution.

• Clean **fibreglass shower trays** and baths with a paste of bicarbonate of soda and washing-up liquid.

• In the unlikely event that you should have some, wipe down **glass shower screens** with left-over white wine.

It goes without saying (I hope) that loos should be cleaned regularly. Don't overdo the chemicals, however, as some of these products are not biodegradable, so add to the problems of breaking down sewage and the pollution of the sea and water courses.

Clean Round the Bend

140

under the rim

Take a look under the rim and you may be unpleasantly surprised at the build-up of limescale and stains. Keep on top of this by using a proprietary cleaner that is thick enough to stay in place and do its job. Apply last thing at night or before going out so it has a few hours to work. Use once or twice a week depending on the amount of toilet traffic.

under the seat

Often neglected, the underside of the loo seat harbours more bacteria than the top. Just don't forget to include it in your cleaning programme.

round the base

Along with under the seat, these two areas are the danger zones and are in most need of attention.

round the bend

Neglect this area and the horrors it harbours soon come creeping out into the open. Avoid limescale build up with specialist loo cleaners, fizzy tablets or chucking a cupful of vinegar down the loo from time to time and leaving over night.

Get Stuck In

The only way to get a loo really clean is to get stuck in. Pull on **rubber gloves** and with a bucket or bowl of **hot sudsy water** sluice down the outside and the seat — both the top and the underside, not forgetting the hinges. Moving on to the inside, enlist the help of a **cream cleanser**, or if you are that way inclined, **bicarbonate of soda** or **borax**. Do a general scrub round with a **toilet brush** and then, using an old **washing-up brush** or **toothbrush**, scrub under the rim. Using the loo brush to push the water round the u-bend, tackle the tidemark. This may involve the use of a **scourer** or toothbrush and/or the application of **specialist limescale remover** or a mix of **borax** and **white vinegar**. Finish with an all-over wash with a weak solution of **warm sudsy water**. Dry the outside and the seat with a clean absorbent cloth.

Now wash
your hands.

143

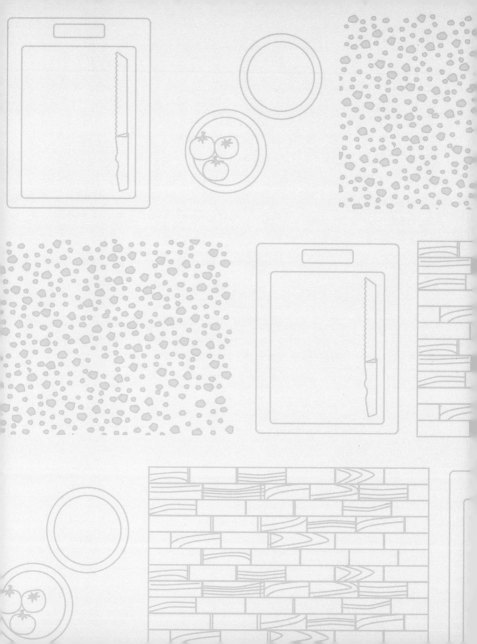

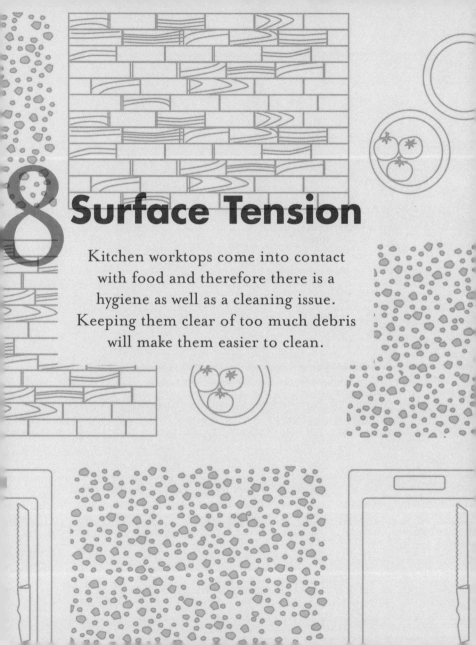

8 Surface Tension

Kitchen worktops come into contact
with food and therefore there is a
hygiene as well as a cleaning issue.
Keeping them clear of too much debris
will make them easier to clean.

Worktop Workout

love that patina

Unless you are a perfection freak or are prepared to spend hours protecting and preserving the 'as new' appearance of your worktop, you are advised to adopt a more pragmatic approach and accept that a well-used worktop will acquire a patina developed over years of use and abuse. By many, this patina is regarded as character.

For most types of worktop a **wipe over** with a cloth wrung out in **warm sudsy water** is enough. Avoid abrasives and don't slosh too much water around as it can soak into joints and joins causing structural damage. Dried-on gunge may require extra effort and an application of **bicarbonate of soda** or a **cream cleaner**.

Protect surfaces by using **chopping boards**: never cut anything directly on the work surface. Not only does it spoil the appearance it also breaks down the surface, which then attracts dirt and bacteria.

Tea and coffee spills stain so use a **tray**.

Never put hot pans or dishes straight from the oven directly on to any type of worktop as the heat causes damage, use **mats or trivets**.

Exceptions and Observations

wood

Make sure any wooden worktop is treated with an oil that will prevent it drying out and increase its waterproofing properties. Scrub occasionally using a nylon mesh scourer dipped in soapy water and follow the grain. Don't allow butchers' block type surfaces to get too wet as they will fall apart – wipe down with a damp cloth then dry thoroughly. Treat the odd dry patch with a little vegetable oil.

laminate

Though hardwearing, these surfaces will stain and scratch. Soak hardened-on goo by placing over a not-too-wet cloth until things soften up. For general staining use an all-purpose liquid cleaner applied with a cloth or soft scourer. Try lemon juice or vinegar on rust and stains.

stone

Natural stone is soluble in acid. Soft versions
including **marble** and **limestone** are more porous
so go steady on the vinegar and acid-based cleaners
and never use lemon on marble stains as it burns
into the surface and the mark cannot be removed.
Granite and **slate** are much harder and more robust
but are still vulnerable to acid attack — and don't
scour them too much as it makes the surface more
porous. With any stone it is important to follow the
manufacturer's care instructions.

Kitchen Killer

One of the most potentially dangerous items in a kitchen is the **chopping board**, which can harbour deadly bacteria as well as insect life.

The greatest danger comes from Salmonella and E.coli often present in un-cooked meat, especially chicken. The bacteria can live on an inadequately washed chopping board where it can be passed on through foodstuffs and on hands.

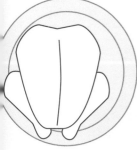

• Avoid the risk of food-poisoning by **using a separate board for meat**. Never chop or place uncooked foodstuffs on a board just used for raw meat.

• After chopping meat **wash the board** in hot, soapy water then soak for 2 minutes in a solution of 3 tablespoons bleach to 1 gallon water, rinse to remove bleach and dry with clean cloth.

• To remove smells **rub with a lemon wedge**, bicarbonate of soda or a vinegar solution.

• Get rid of stains by **sprinkling with salt** or rubbing with lemon or a paste of bicarbonate of soda.

• **Butchers' block boards** will split if soaked so wipe them down with a bleach solution then wipe several times with clean water and dry well.

9 Appliance Science

Even modest homes now have
an impressive number of appliances
to help us get through our busy days.
It's tempting to think they look after
themselves, but in fact they need
cleaning and maintenance to keep
them in working order.

Cook's Dilemma

If you survive on takeaways or ready-meals, the most important item to keep clean will be the microwave. If you cook proper meals, your hob, oven and kitchen will get grubby from all the steam and grease, splashes and spills.

There are no easy miracle cleaners, so the best course of action is to be very organised and disciplined.

hob habit

Get into the habit of wiping down the hob immediately after use. A **damp cloth** should be enough but always finish with a **clean cloth** otherwise some food may be left behind, which will harden when the heat is next on. Avoid abrasive cleaners and for hardened-on spills squeeze on a spongeful of **warm sudsy water** or cover with a soaked cloth, leave for at least an hour before wiping off with **clean cloth** or nylon scourer. Some fastidious fussers put **aluminium foil** underneath the burners, but frankly it looks horrible and as well as being an extravagant use of foil.

If, despite solicitous soaking and scrubbing, the marks persist you may have to resort to a **commercial miracle cleaning spray** – and then resolve to develop the hob habit.

Oven Heaven

Wiping down the oven after each cooking session is, of course, the best way of keeping the oven clean, but once the oven door is closed it's easy to forget about it. If done fairly frequently it can be cleaned using **hot water** with a good squirt of **washing-up liquid** and a **nylon scourer** (avoid wire wool as it scratches), resorting to a mildly abrasive cream for stubborn stuff. If you are a once-a-year oven cleaner you will have to resort to **specialist oven cleaners** that are effective but highly toxic. Follow the instructions very carefully, wear rubber gloves, protect floors and other nearby surfaces and make sure there is plenty of ventilation.

Clean dirty **oven shelves** by immersing in a mixture of 1 part washing soda to 4 parts hot water.

To freshen up a **microwave** place a few slices of lemon in a bowl of cold water, heat, uncovered to boiling point on high, cook on high for 60 seconds.

Fridges and Freezers

Fridges and freezers will work more efficiently if they are defrosted regularly. Don't forget to check the temperature — no warmer than 4°C for the fridge and -18°C for the freezer.

quick once over

• Fridges get neglected and sometimes it is only when you look closely you see the fingermarks on the outside and the drips, bits and blobs of gunge on the inside. Keep things fresh with a regular clean.

• Take out all shelves, drawers and removable storage parts before washing

• Wash down the outside and inside using a cloth and warm water with a small squirt of washing-up liquid. Pay attention to the outlet pipe, which may have gathered gunge and become partially blocked and pop in a little bicarbonate of soda to help sluice it out.

• Wipe down the shelves with a cloth or, if they are very grubby, wash them in a sink full of sudsy water.

• Finish the inside by wiping down with a weak vinegar and water solution, which will freshen the atmosphere.

• Dry everything thoroughly using a soft, dry cloth.

• If possible pull the fridge away from the wall and remove the dust on the metal grille using a vacuum cleaner or damp cloth.

• Clean out the drip tray – soak up the water and any mouldy gunge with a cloth or paper towels, wipe clean and dry thoroughly.

Don't bother with expensive
fridge deodorisers; a small bowl
of bicarbonate of soda in the fridge
will absorb any strong smells.

Kettles and Co.

Commercial de-scalers are fine for cleaning **kettles**, but a cheaper alternative is vinegar. For an uncovered element, pour in enough vinegar to cover and top up with water. For a concealed element, use 100–150ml vinegar. Bring to the boil and leave overnight.

To clean **food mixers and blenders** after use add 1 teaspoon washing-up liquid to 200ml warm water and whizz for 30 seconds.

Crumbs left in a **toaster** will burn and taint the toast. Unplug the toaster, empty the crumb tray or, if there isn't one, hold the toaster upside-down over a bin, give it a good tap to get everything out. Use a small pastry brush or soft toothbrush to gently brush debris off the elements.

When grinding coffee beans, there is always a little left behind in a **coffee grinder**. Over time it will go stale and taint any new coffee. Use an artist's brush to remove it, but unplug the appliance first.

Dishwasher Discipline

Dishwashers are great. They keep the kitchen tidy and get things a lot cleaner than most humans. And the good news for eco-warriors is that they are not as wasteful on water as you might expect. They work well if you follow the manufacturer's instructions, but it is surprising how dirty they can get. Empty and clean the filters regularly and give door seals a regular wipe down with warm sudsy water. If you live in a hard water area, make sure the salt reservoir is regularly topped up.

• **Freshen up** by placing a shallow bowl of vinegar (150–200ml) in the bottom rack and run through a wash cycle.

• To remove **milky film** from glassware put a bowl in the bottom of the dishwasher filled with household bleach and run through a wash cycle but do not dry. Fill a bowl with vinegar and run through an entire cycle.

• Treat **odours** by sprinkling borax in the bottom and leave overnight then wipe down the inside. There is no need to rinse, just do next load.

163

164

Washing Machines

The washing machine is a wonderful invention and deserves to be looked after.

The **detergent dispenser** gets very gungy and clogged so take it out, immerse it in hot sudsy water and give it a good clean. A toothbrush is useful for getting into the nooks and crannies.

Before putting it back in, clean the **detergent dispenser's space**. You may be horrified to see how much sticky detergent and softener has accumulated. New soap powders, tablets and liquids are formulated for use at low temperatures. Whilst this is good for energy conservation and fabrics, the water is not hot enough to kill a number of **bacteria and moulds**, resulting in a smelly washing machine. To cure this do a 90°C wash (an opportunity to wash all those old towels and cloths) at least once a month.

Limescale build-up damages the machine as well as impairing performance (see page 118). If hard water is a problem, use commercial water-softeners that can be used with each wash or use a stronger limescale remover at regular intervals.

10 Laundry List

How often you change the bedlinen depends on your standards and circumstances, but even if you sleep alone and always bathe or shower before bed remember all those dead skin cells and sweat — and even prim and proper people dribble in their sleep.

Soap Opera

The good news is that modern detergents are so efficient that, provided you follow the instructions, they even remove what used to be regarded as 'stubborn stains'.

They come in powder, concentrated powder, tablet and liquid form and whichever you choose depends on the state of the washing, personal preference and what works best in your machine.

• **Biological detergents** contain enzymes, which break down dirt and make a meal of stains. However, they also contain chemicals that can provoke allergic reactions and skin irritations.
• **Non-bio** alternatives are less harsh and kinder to the skin but less effective on super stains.
• **Eco-friendly** detergents are kind to people, the planet and your washing, but are not always brilliant at tackling dirt and stains.

soft options

The world of fabric softeners can be a confusing one but their primary function is to soften fibres and remove any detergent residue. Many contain a cocktail of chemicals and artificial perfumes so if you don't want that sort of thing stick to the eco-versions. Alternatively, add a couple of tablespoons of white vinegar to the final rinse.

CONTAMINATION ALERT!

If, despite your best efforts, a rogue black sock or green t-shirt has tinted and tainted your whites, remove the offending article and wash the load again (and again if the damage is great) using a biological detergent. If the problem persists, try using a powdered laundry bleach in with the load or soaking in mild bleach or a specialist commercial product. The bleaching effects of sunshine can also help.

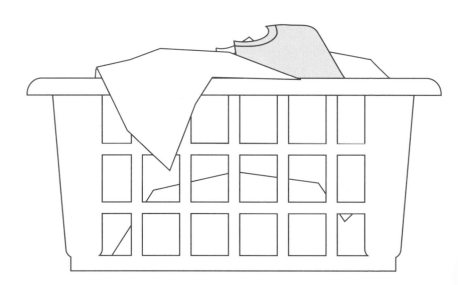

Washing Instructions

• **Read** each garment's label and follow the recommended washing instructions.

• **Measure** the detergent and softener and use as directed on the packet.

• **Sort** your washing into piles according to colour, temperature and fabric type.

• **Keep** whites white by washing in a whites-only load.

• **Don't overload** the machine and make sure that items are loaded loosely and not bundled together.

• **Do a smaller load** if stuff is very grubby to allow room for agitation.

• **Use more detergent** in hard water areas if necessary – see the detergent label for details.

• **Fasten** poppers, ties and buttons on duvet covers to stop other items getting inside and forming a ball that will send your washing machine into a noisy spin.

• **Minimise** any irritating effects of a biological detergent by doing an extra rinse.

Dry Conditions

Tumble driers are useful, especially if you have nowhere to hang things out to dry. However, they are expensive to run and the heat and tumbling can damage fabrics and reduce their life expectancy.

Whatever drying method you use, always shake out or pull items into shape, especially along seams and embroidered sections, as this makes ironing easier. Don't pull too hard as you could break the stitching.

outdoors

A long, **single washing line** is best, but if space is restricted the **rotary clothes line** is fine though stuff on the inside will not dry so quickly.

Use **plastic washing line** and before using clean it by running a damp cloth along it.

Hang **sheets** up by the hems rather than draping them over the line, they will dry more quickly.

Sunshine fades **bright colours** so unless you want the shabby chic look dry away from direct sun.

indoors

When drying clothes indoors, avoid creating **damp problems** by ensuring the drying area is well ventilated. By an open window or sunny spot is best.

There is a huge variety of **clothes airers** on the market and the choice depends on cost, space, looks and personal preference, but avoid un-treated wooden racks as they can stain the washing.

Avoid folding items and **overcrowding racks** as they will take longer to dry and may become smelly. Rails that hook over radiators provide extra, quick-drying space.

The old-fashioned 'dolly' clothes airers that hang from ceilings look great and make the most of heat rising, but bear in mind that if you put one in the **kitchen** the washing will absorb cooking smells.

Tumbling Tips

• Remove any fluff from the drier's filter either before or after every use.

• Make sure the drier is vented to the outside as the moisture will cause damp problems in your home.

• Don't overload as this leads to uneven drying.

• Don't mix different fibres as some dry quicker than others.

• Don't over-dry items as it makes them more difficult to iron.

• Get rid of any hairs and bits of tissues by tumble drying the affected items for 10 minutes on a cool setting.

• Make things smell nice by putting a handkerchief sprinkled with your favourite essential oil or perfume in with the load.

Between the Sheets

The smell and feel of clean sheets is one of life's little pleasures and if you need an excuse, or a prod, to change the bed here are a few facts and fixes.

- Eschew 'easy-care' synthetic fibres, you can't beat **pure cotton or linen** for comfort.
- You can **save on washing** by changing just the bottom bed sheet and pillowcases and turning the duvet over.
- Even if you aren't changing all the bed linen, **clean pillowcases** will feel good.
- **Use a flat sheet**, which is less bulky to wash, between you and the duvet.
- Turn flat bottom sheets into fitted sheets by **tying a knot** in each corner.
- Change all bedlinen after any illness. To kill any bugs, **wash at minimum 60°C** and iron on a high temperature.
- If you have an infection or are fighting spots with medication **change your pillowcase** frequently to avoid any remaining bacteria causing re-infection.

Curtains and Covers

Because laundering is more thorough and involves fewer chemicals than dry cleaning (and is a lot cheaper), it's a good idea wherever possible to opt for machine-washable curtaining, cushion covers, blankets and throws. Washing reduces the damaging effects of dirt and dust but these items don't need doing very often especially if you shake the dust out or vacuum frequently. Allow plenty of room for these bulky items to slosh around in the suds, do small loads and if necessary use an extra large machine at the laundrette. Use a cool wash cycle and only tumble dry if there is a cool cycle and plenty of room, otherwise they might shrink and will crease.

quick freshen-up

- Vacuum curtains to keep down the dust.
- Give curtains a few hours outside on a breezy, sunny day.
- Hang curtains in a steamy environment — just after your bath or shower, this freshens them up and is very good for perking up velvet.
- Put them in the tumble drier with a few fabric softener sheets for the cool 10 minutes at the end of a cycle.

Fabric Stains

The wonders of new detergents mean that a lot of stains that would previously have needed special attention magically disappear in the wash. The more stubborn varieties of stains may need **several washes** or a **pre-soak** in a solution of detergent (make sure the detergent has dissolved properly) or an application of **neat detergent** on the affected area. Even if you don't use it normally, keep some biological washing detergent ready for emergencies. Treatment will be more effective if you take **immediate action** diluting the stain with water — preferably with bubbles.

stain reaction

- **tea and coffee** — rinse out the worst and wash immediately
- **red wine** — dilute with white wine or water and wash as soon as possible
- **blood** — apply neat biological laundry detergent and leave for a while before washing
- **red fruit** — if you have a steady hand stretch the

stained area over a bucket or bowl and pour on boiling water from a great height, then soak in 1 part vinegar to 2 parts water. Otherwise use biological detergent and hope it fades over time

• **curry** — a tricky one but the yellow turmeric stain (the main culprit) can be treated by rubbing with methylated spirit on a clean cloth before washing. It may take some time to fade but will be helped by exposure to sunlight

• **lipstick** — if bio-detergent doesn't work use a proprietry stain remover

• **wax** — put the item in the freezer overnight (for big items put a freezer pack on the affected part). Chip off excess wax then place the fabric (wax side down) between two pieces of kitchen towel and apply a warm iron. If some wax remains rub in a little vegetable oil allow to sit for 10–15 minutes and blot before washing

try not to rub stains too much as it pushes
the stain further into the fabric

182

Delicates Operation

When washing delicate fabrics use a gentle detergent, either an eco-variety or a product specially formulated for delicates. Washing by hand may be best but a machine wash is more thorough. Use a gentle, low-temperature programme and place small, more fragile items inside a pillowcase.

Old cottons and linens can be whitened by soaking in a mild bleach solution though they will usually whiten with frequent washing. Follow the same procedure for mildew stains or soak in a bucket with two denture tablets. Remember that sunlight is also an effective bleach and stain remover.

Getting Steamed Up

5 good reasons for doing the ironing

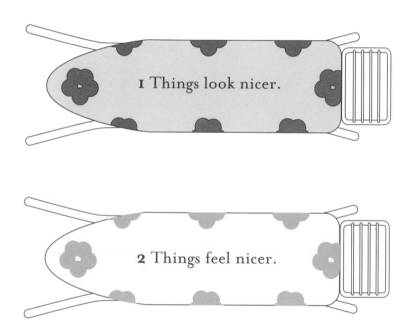

1 Things look nicer.

2 Things feel nicer.

3 Ironing makes fabrics more dirt-resistant.

4 It's a guilt-free way to spend time watching TV.

5 A hot iron kills bugs and bacteria in towels, linens etc.

Tips for Iron Maidens

• **Gently pulling** into shape and **neatly folding** dry washing minimises creasing and makes ironing easier.

• **Folding sheets** and large cloths double makes them easier to handle. Iron one side, fold with the pressed side on the inside and continue ironing and folding until you have a neat, folded, fully ironed item.

• Keep large items **off the floor** by draping the ironed bit over the back of a chair positioned behind the ironing board.

• Using **distilled water** in a steam iron prevents the build up of limescale. Alternatively, use filtered water from a **filter jug**.

• **De-scale** a steam iron by filling with a solution of 1 part water to 1 part vinegar. Steam for a few minutes, allow to cool, then rinse with clear water.

• Prolong the life of a new **ironing board cover** by liberally spraying it with **spray starch** followed by a good hot ironing.

• Clean the **base** of the iron with a damp cloth dipped in **bicarbonate of soda**.

• Better results will be achieved if you **iron things while damp**, if you are not going to iron straight away put them in a plastic bag in the fridge to stop them going smelly.

• **Linen sprays** make ironing a more pleasurable experience. If you can't afford the posh versions, make your own by adding a few drops of lavender or another favourite essential oil to a spray bottle filled with water.

If you hate ironing, follow the fashion for shabby chic where creases are de rigeur. It's not the end of the world if your sheets are un-ironed. When bedlinens are dry, pull into shape, fold carefully and place at the bottom of the linen pile to flatten them.

Laundry List

Air Time

There was a time when if you went to bed in un-aired bedclothes you were thought to be putting your life in danger. Nowadays we tend not to think about such things but while not exactly life-threatening, damp bedclothes are to be avoided. Items that have been steam-ironed require airing before use so if you only have one set of sheets try to wash, dry and iron them in the morning to allow for airing time – or save up for a second set.

Fewer homes now have an 'airing-cupboard' so use a clothes airer in a warm dry place, hang items over a radiator rail or place on a sunny windowsill for at least an hour, preferably more.

put it away

The ideal of impressive quantities of perfectly folded, colour co-ordinated linens and towels neatly stacked inside an equally impressive large cupboard or linen press and topped with bunches of freshly picked lavender is seductive if not always achievable. You may not have such illustrious facilities but a drawer or shelf in the wardrobe will suffice as long as it is dry. Alternatively what about a wooden chest or a wicker basket? And don't forget the lavender.

• White bedlinen and towels can go **yellowy** over time so if you are lucky enough to have piles of them make sure you **rotate** them by always putting the clean ones at the bottom.

• Line drawers with paper — treat yourself to scented drawer liners otherwise use brown paper or wallpaper sprayed with essential oils, bunches of lavender and herbs, or leave old perfume bottles between the sheets.

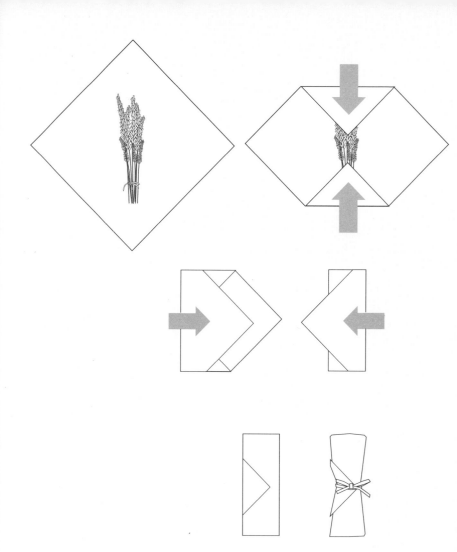

Pretty Pastime

With lavender and herbs growing in nearly every trendy garden don't let them go to waste. If you fancy sewing lavender bags and herb sachets go ahead, but if you are not nifty with a needle wrap them up and tie with ribbon, string or even a rubber band. Use fine muslin which lets the smell out but stops the herbs shedding bits and prevents possible staining. As a change from lavender use cloves, cinnamon sticks and orange peel.

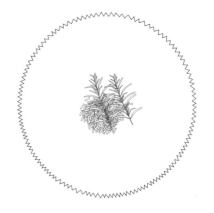

II Flawless Floors

A dirty floor makes your whole home look dirty even if it isn't. Neglecting floors is a bit like spoiling a smart outfit by wearing scruffy shoes.

Carpet Care

Clean carpets are great, those covered in bits and fluff detract from even the most stunning decor and dirty ones just look disgusting. All carpets and rugs will benefit from regular attention.

- **vacuum** once or twice a week
- **mop up** any spills immediately
- **place** doormats at entrance points to prevent dirt being trodden through

Follow the manufacturer's instructions for special weaves and fibres and don't use a rotating brush on natural floorcoverings such as sisal and seagrass as this will destroy the surface fibres.

quick carpet spring clean

1 Remove as much of the furniture as possible.
2 Vacuum the carpet thoroughly paying attention to edges and corners.
3 Tackle any obvious marks using a clean cloth wrung out in warm water plus a squeeze of washing-up liquid, or a suitable solvent for bad stains.
4 Repeat using clean water.
5 Allow to dry (you may want to do this the day before to make sure the stained patches are thoroughly dry).
5 Sprinkle a proprietary dry powder shampoo generously all over the carpet
6 Brush the powder into the pile using a clean stiff brush.
7 Leave for the length of time recommended on the instructions.
8 Vacuum thoroughly.
9 Use a stiff brush to raise the pile (optional).

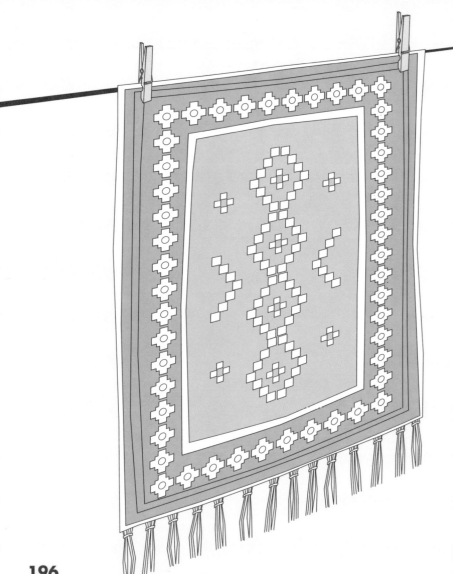

196

Beat That

A good bashing is brilliant for getting the dust out of rugs, kelims and dhurries. Hang them over a washing line or pole (but make sure it is up to the job) and beat them using a carpet beater (if you can find one) or a broom.

The rugs (and you) will enjoy it.

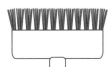

Carpet Stains

mild solution

A lot of carpet stains can be removed quite successfully if they are treated immediately with the stain emergency routine: blotting, diluting, washing with a mild detergent solution followed by rinsing with clean water and lots of blotting dry using clean, dry cloths. Spills of coffee and tea, white wine, blood, food (except curry), cola and other soft drinks should respond well to this treatment as long as it is done promptly but others may require something stronger.

stronger solutions

• **vinegar** – 1 part vinegar to 3 parts water, apply with a sponge or cloth
• **white spirit** – use neat on a clean cloth
• **commercial carpet stain remover** – read and follow the instructions carefully. Apply on a clean cloth or a spare sample piece of the carpet

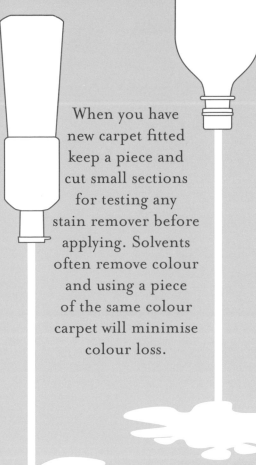

When you have
new carpet fitted
keep a piece and
cut small sections
for testing any
stain remover before
applying. Solvents
often remove colour
and using a piece
of the same colour
carpet will minimise
colour loss.

stronger methods

Follow the mild solution with further action:

• **chocolate**, **ketchup** and **red fruit** stains may need a specialist stain remover
• **red wine** – don't put salt on it, blot instead with white wine or water followed by stain remover, if necessary
• **grease** – try the vinegar solution or white spirit
• **glue** and **solvent-based paint** – white spirit on a piece of carpet or dry cloth
• **oil** and **tar** – dissolve and remove using eucalyptus oil on a clean cloth followed by the mild solution treatment
• **vomit** – mop or scrape up (a cake slice is useful) as quickly as possible as stomach acids damage and bleach out colour. If the mild solution doesn't work try vinegar or stain remover
• **chewing gum** – harden using a freezer pack, chip off and dig out. If that doesn't work soften the gum with a little petroleum jelly and ease it off the fibres using your fingers

- **wax** – harden and chip off surplus wax using a freezer pack as above. Remove any remaining wax using brown or kitchen paper and a warm iron (a small travel iron is ideal), taking care to use a large enough area of paper to prevent accidently burning the carpet
- **trodden-in dirt** often looks much worse than it is. Allow it to dry, vacuum up then use further stain-removal treatment as necessary
- for natural fibres such as **sisal**, **jute** and **seagrass**, blot up any spills immediately and treat serious stains with specialist products as recommended or supplied by the manufacturer and fitter. A cocktail stick is useful for digging out bits of spilt food or dirt
- **scorch marks** – difficult to remedy but trimming the damaged ends with scissors will make them less noticeable

Bare Essentials

Looking after bare floors is relatively simple and straightforward especially if you follow a simple, regular routine.

sweeping

Dust may look harmless but it usually contains bits of dirt that get ground into the floor and damage the surface. It's important, therefore to clean floors regularly even if it's just a quick sweep. Use a fine, soft bristled broom and/or a dustpan and brush.

vacuuming

Vacuuming is a good way to clean bare floors but be careful – big pieces of dirt and grit may get caught under the cleaner and scratch the floor so use a soft brush specialist floor attachment. Use the thin, pointy attachment to get into corners, gaps, edges and the tops of skirting boards.

wet mopping

Most hard floors can be cleaned by mopping with warm, sudsy water as long as you are careful not to over-wet the floor. Vinyl, linoleum, stone, tiles, laminates, painted and solid wood can be mopped but if you have a new, posh floor follow the installer's instructions.

dry mopping and damp dusting

After a sweep, some floors, especially waxed ones, need only a quick buffing either with a dry duster tied round a dry mop or a slightly dampened duster, which also picks up a certain amount of surface dirt.

There are lots of wonder floor treatments around but use with caution as many leave residues that build up over time to form a dull, unattractive finish, which may also absorb extra dirt.

How to Mop a Floor

1 **Make** sure the mop and the bucket are clean.

2 **Fill** the bucket with warm water plus either a squeeze of washing-up liquid or the prescribed amount of general purpose surface or floor cleaner – make sure the water comes well below the bit where you squeeze the mop.

3 **Dip** the mop in the water and squeeze out well; you don't want water sloshing around especially on laminates where excess water can cause the surface to lift.

4 **Start** in one corner and mop the floor in front of you making sure you get into the corners and edges. On tiled floors don't forget the grouting between the tiles.

5 Dip and squeeze at regular intervals. Don't do too much with one mop-full otherwise you will be spreading the dirt around rather than removing it.

6 Change the water in the bucket as soon as it looks obviously dirty.

7 Empty the bucket, rinse out, fill with clean, hot water and rinse out the mop.

8 Empty the bucket again, refill with clean, warm water and, squeezing as much water as possible out of the mop, go over the whole floor again – this may seem a bit of an effort but you may be surprised to see how much more dirt you pick up.

School for Scrubbers

Getting down on your hands and knees to give the floor a good scrub can leave you, and the floor, remarkably refreshed. It's more thorough and can even be quicker and easier than mopping, especially in a confined space such as a bathroom, loo or small kitchen.

1 Pull on your rubber gloves and get a kneeler —
either purpose-made or a folded towel.

2 Fill a bucket with warm water and add a squeeze
of washing-up liquid or all-purpose surface or
floor cleaner.

3 Dip a large, absorbent cotton or linen cloth (or
soft scrubbing brush) into the water, squeeze out
and start cleaning, rubbing briskly and paying
attention to corners and edges and changing the
water as soon as it gets very dirty.

4 Tackle tough dirt and hardened-on bits using
a nylon scourer with neat cleaning product
wherever necessary.

5 Use a scrubbing brush or toothbrush to clean the
grouting between the tiles.

6 Wipe over the just-cleaned section with the cloth
squeezed out more thoroughly.

7 Repeat the process using clean warm water.

8 Dry off with a soft, absorbent cloth (you may
need more than one).

Bare Facts

- **Waxed floors** look wonderful but wax absorbs dirt and a build-up dulls the surface so apply wax only once or twice a year, depending on the amount of foot traffic. The same goes for **oiled finishes**.
- Never put wax on **varnished or laminate finishes**, it won't be absorbed.
- Remove **marks and scuffs** with a damp cloth and a little bicarbonate of soda or liquid cleaner.
- Use very fine wire wool to tackle ingrained **dirt and scratches** on **wooden or stone floors**.
- Soft stones, such as **limestone and marble**, are mostly calcium, which is soluble in acid so don't use harsh cleaners. Use a mild detergent solution and avoid soap products as they form a scummy layer.
- Scrape **chewing gum** off with a palette knife and rub the residue off with fine wire wool.

interesting fact

Stone is soft when dug out of the ground, but hardens on exposure to air and foot traffic and forms a hard, self-cleaning surface over time.

safety alert

Shiny floors may look wonderful
but they can be treacherously slippery
to even the most sure-footed and
sober soul.

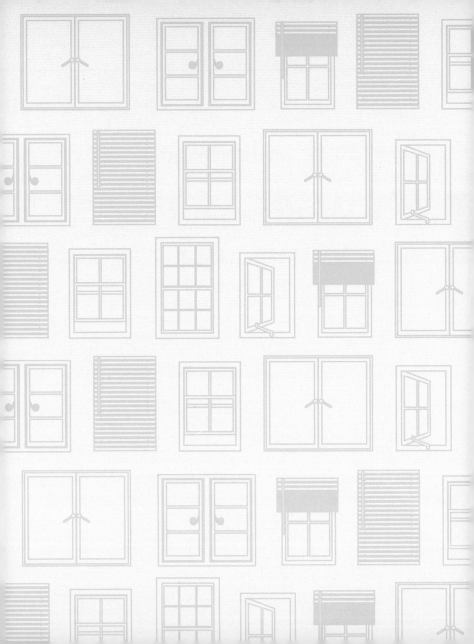

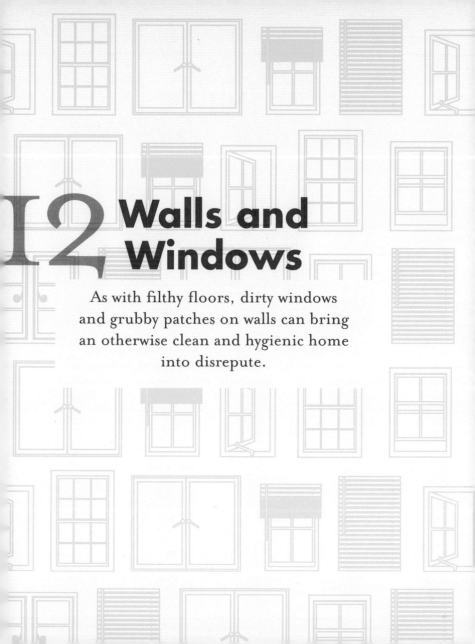

12 Walls and Windows

As with filthy floors, dirty windows and grubby patches on walls can bring an otherwise clean and hygienic home into disrepute.

When You're Cleaning Windows

Forget special window cleaning products and all that newspaper and vinegar stuff — the best way to clean windows is with a mild detergent solution. Windows will only look really clean if they are done inside and out, but be careful if you are climbing on ladders or windowsills — safety is more important than cleanliness so far better to pay your friendly neighbourhood window cleaner to reach the parts the safety-conscious occupant cannot reach.

- Put the sudsy solution into a spray bottle – it's easier to handle than a bucket.

- Don't wash windows on sunny days, they dry too quickly and go streaky.

- Wipe up and down on one side and side to side on the other so that when, inevitably, you spot a few streaks you know whether they are on the inside or outside.

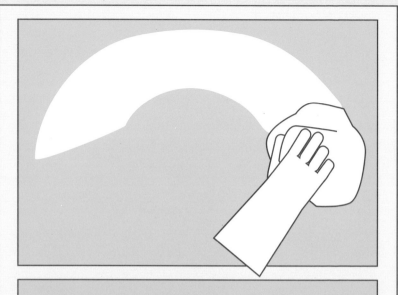

one way for windows

• **Place** a towel or absorbent cloth on the windowsill to protect the paintwork from water.
• **Start** at the top and apply sudsy water (warm water plus a squeeze of washing-up liquid) with a cloth or sponge scourer (the soft sort) making sure you get into the corners.
• **Wipe** off any surplus with a wrung-out cloth.
• **Repeat** using clean water.
• **Dry** and buff with a soft, lint-free cloth.

another way for windows

• **Apply** sudsy water as before, then finish with one of those special window-cleaning squeegees.

• **Remember** to start at the top, don't forget the corners and have a dry cloth handy to wipe the drips from the squeegee.

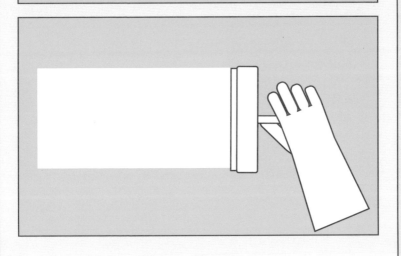

Blinding Light

5 ways to clean a slatted blind

with gloves

Dust the blinds by hand wearing cotton household gloves (available in all good cleaning departments). Brush off the dust as you go. For more neglected blinds dip your gloved hands into mild detergent solution, squeeze out excess water and get cleaning.

special implement

There are many specialist gadgets, some of them quite ingenious allowing you to clean several slats at once. As with gloves shake dust off frequently and wash after use.

hair drier or vacuum cleaner

A quick blast with the hair dryer can dislodge light coverings of dust. But don't forget to collect up the dust from where it has settled. Alternatively, use a vacuum cleaner with an appropriate attachment.

shower or bath

Clean plastic or metal blinds in the shower or bath using the shower attachment. A few squirts of spray cleaner helps cut through grease. Alternatively, hang outside on the washing line and use the garden hose.

on the floor

If it is easy to take down and you have enough room, spread out the blind on the floor with the slats closed. Clean using a duster, vacuum cleaner or damp cloth (or all three). Turn over and clean the other side.

roller blinds

If you have wipe-clean roller blinds then go ahead and wipe them clean using a damp cloth and, if necessary, a little detergent. For fabric blinds dust regularly and thoroughly, using a duster or vacuum cleaner. Most roller blinds are treated to make the fabric stiffer so tackle stains with care. Try the gentle water and detergent method of removal, but follow the manufacturer's instructions and when in doubt use a proprietary stain remover.

Extra-Mural Studies

It is surprising how much dust settles on **walls**. Remove it using a long-handled feather duster or brush, or with a broom or dry mop with a clean duster tied round the head.

Wash down **paintwork** on doors, door and window frames, skirting boards and picture or dado rails with a cloth or sponge and mild detergent solution. Don't use anything stronger and don't use scourers as this will destroy the surface and make it less dirt resistant. Afterwards, dry thoroughly.

Wash **dirty patches** with a damp cloth wrung out in warm, weak detergent solution. Don't rub too hard as this will remove the paint. Use a paste or solution of bicarbonate of soda for stubborn and greasy stains.

Freshen-up **stained areas** behind work surfaces, sinks, cookers and bedheads by washing down then re-painting with watered-down paint (1 part paint to 2 parts water). It may be necessary to do the whole wall otherwise it could look patchy.

If **damp and mildew stains** defy your attempts to remove them, paint the wall with a proprietary sealant or primer and then re-paint.

If budding young artists have been **drawing on walls**, a soft eraser is the obvious choice to remove pencil marks.

For **crayon marks** try bicarbonate of soda on a cloth, or a lubricant spray, such as WD-40™, onto the crayon, wipe off and wash the area with warm sudsy water.

Wallpaper

Whereas paint can be washed down wallpaper needs gentler treatment. For **washable wallpapers** wipe down with a **damp cloth** but remember to follow the manufacturer's instructions.

Remove **dirty marks** on wallpapers with **white bread** gently squeezed into a ball – good-old white sliced is best. You can also use an **eraser** – the art gum type is best as it crumbles as you use it and doesn't smear.

Remove **grease spots** by ironing on top of **brown paper or kitchen paper** placed over the mark. You could also try dusting with **talcum powder**: leave for a couple of hours before brushing off with a soft brush.

Remove **adhesive tape** with a **warm iron** – not on steam! – which will soften the glue and allow you to peel the tape off.

a small travel iron is much easier to handle and minimises the risk of damaging the surrounding wallpaper

Paper
Patchwork

Worn areas, tears and bad stains can be repaired and hidden with a patch – providing you have some left-over wallpaper. Straight-cut edges will stand out, however, whereas torn edges will not, so tear out a piece slightly bigger than the damaged area – not forgetting to match up the pattern. Brush on some wallpaper paste, making sure the edges are well pasted. Place over the damaged area, slide into place to match the pattern and smooth down, starting at the centre, using a decorator's brush or soft dry cloth. If the colour looks too new and bright try 'ageing' the patch by dabbing with a damp cloth dipped in very weak tea or gently rubbing in a little dust from a duster.

13 Furniture Polish

Furnishings will look better and
last longer if you look after them.
Most care involves nothing more than
dust removal, the odd wipe down and
a bit of buffing, but an accident or
serious case of neglect may require
a little more attention.

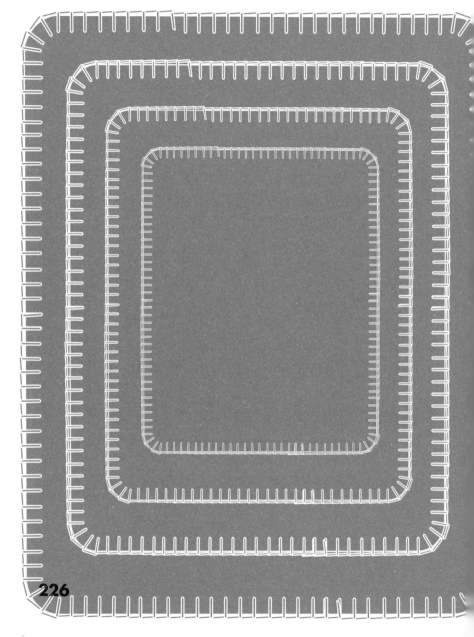

226

Buffer's Guide

Cleaning instructions often recommend a good buffing, a process that produces a satisfying glow on furniture, surfaces and, if you work hard enough, your own face.

Proper buffing requires good lint-free cloths — linen or cotton, woven not knitted and soft not scratchy – plus a fair amount of energy.

• First of all, remove any dust and surface dirt using a damp cloth.
• Allow everything to dry before rubbing briskly, making sure you get into every corner, nook and cranny.
• For extra power, fold or gather the cloth so that it forms a small, thick wad enabling you to apply more concentrated pressure.
• When buffing wood, always go with the grain.

Furniture Polish

Wood Care

Wood matures, darkens and mellows over time, especially if it is treated well.

varnished wood

Most new wood used in furniture is sealed with a varnish and therefore needs only a wipe over with the proverbial damp cloth and perhaps a small amount of detergent for sticky marks and dirt.

Don't use a scourer or any abrasives as this will break down the surface allowing in dirt and moisture.

waxed wood

Dust regularly, wipe off dirt with a damp cloth. Wax once a year but don't put more wax on top of dirty wax – wax doesn't clean, it seals.

painted wood

Clean off marks with a damp cloth or wash down with a mild detergent, finish with a cloth squeezed out in clean water and dry thoroughly.

Protect and bring a glow to non-gloss paint finishes with an application of wax polish well buffed up.

To remove a build-up of excess
wax, rub with I part vinegar
to I part water and
dry immediately.

On Your Marks

• Put **petroleum jelly** on rings left by cups and glasses, leave for 24 hours and then wipe off.

• Use a small amount of **non-gel toothpaste** on a clean cloth and rub till the mark has gone.

• Neat **liquid-cream metal polish** applied with a clean cloth should help get rid of any heat and water marks.

• Disguise scratches with **crayons**, **boot polish** or, on dark woods such as mahogany and cherry, **iodine**. Apply sparingly on a clean cloth or cotton wool.

Furniture Polish

New Lease of Life

Bring a glow back to tired, dry-looking, stripped pine or waxed wood with a wash and buff up.

1 **Wash** down with a damp cloth and warm water with a small squirt of washing-up liquid (or a proprietary wood wash). Use a soft scourer on obvious dirt. Finish with a wipe-over using clean water.

2 **Wipe** off as much moisture as possible with a soft, lint-free cloth.

3 **Leave** to dry thoroughly.

4 **Apply** liquid wax or furniture oil on a soft cloth, applying evenly to avoid patches.

5 **Rub** off any surplus, following the instructions regarding drying time.

6 **Buff** vigorously.

smooth running

Cure squeaky hinges and loosen stiff catches with a squirt of fine spray oil, using the thin nozzle to get to the heart of the problem.

If your drawers are sticking, rub the runners with the wax from a candle.

Liquid waxes and furniture oils are available in different wood colours so make sure you choose the right one.

It's best to stick to pale colours or, in the case of oil, colourless. If the liquid wax has hardened, soften it up by standing the tin in a jug of hot water.

Leather

New leather furniture normally comes complete with manufacturers' care instructions so put them in a safe place and follow them carefully. Don't get paranoid about the odd mark and scratch and accept that leather matures with use and acquires a patina that most people think improves both the look and the feel.

• If possible, keep leather out of **direct sunlight**, which dries it out and makes it crack. Dust frequently and unless otherwise instructed, clean off marks with a **damp cloth**.
• For **serious marks** on leather wipe a cloth over a bar of **moisturising soap**, rub the leather clean and then buff off.
• An occasional application of **hide food or saddle soap** will restore life and colour. Do what it says on the tin and buff well. If you are into shabby chic and love the look of old leather, even if it is torn and worn, this treatment will slow the process of deterioration.

Plastic Fantastic

Plastic and acrylic furniture looks fabulous when new, but it is difficult to retain that shiny finish. Frequent dusting and buffing will minimise surface damage but accept that the surface will, in time, become softer, duller but more mellow.

Wipe plastics and acrylics down occasionally with a damp cloth and for dirty marks try a small amount of neat washing-up liquid. Never use harsh abrasives or scourers.

For scratches on acrylics try rubbing in a small amount of non-gel toothpaste, buffing until the toothpaste, and hopefully the scratch, have disappeared.

Table Top Tips

Glass table tops are vulnerable to scratching so always use **tablecloths and mats**. Clean off smears and grease with a **damp cloth and sudsy water** and polish dry. Polishing with a little **methylated spirit** on a clean cloth removes grease and retains sparkle. You can try removing scratches using **non-gel toothpaste**. Chips can be filed down using a **fine emery paper**, but be careful not to damage the surrounding surface – or your fingers.

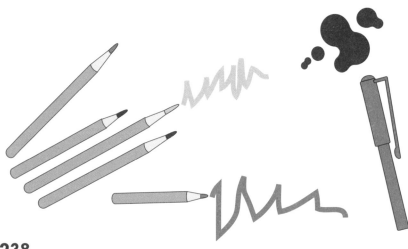

desk top polishing

Most of us now have a work area in our homes complete with home computer and related equipment. Keeping equipment on a **mat** – a place mat or small cotton dhurry, depending on the size of the item – protects surfaces from damage and allows you to slide things around for cleaning.

A non-abrasive, **all-purpose surface cleaner** can remove **ink and felt-tip pen** (but not indelible versions) from laminates or varnished wood.

Rubber-based **white glue** can be removed with **warm suds**; don't scour, just wait for it to dissolve.

Carefully scrape off blobs of **solvent-based glues** with a small paint scraper and dissolve any remaining residue with **white spirit or nail-polish remover** which is, of course, also the best thing for removing spilled **nail varnish**.

Upholstery

If your sofas and armchairs are looking tired and a bit grubby perk them up with a little TLC.

fixed covers

1 **Take** off any loose seat and back cushions and give them a good plumping.

2 **Vacuum** the cushions and frame using a brush attachment and the narrow nozzle tool to get down the sides and backs.

3 **Wipe** over with a barely damp cloth, wrung out in clean water.

4 **Tackle** stains with a damp cloth and warm water with a little washing-up liquid. Resort to a proprietary stain remover if necessary.

loose covers

• The great thing about loose covers is that they can be taken off and washed or dry-cleaned. However, getting them on and off can require quite an effort so if they are not too dirty freshen them up as for fixed covers.

• If you do remove them follow the manufacturer's washing or cleaning instructions carefully.

• Because covers are big and bulky it's best to wash them in a big machine at the launderette. When you take them out, pull them into shape and dry them naturally as tumble drying tends to shrink fabrics.

• The shapes can be awkward but ironing helps to keep the fabric clean and, if you are careful, you can always run the iron over them after they have been put back on.

Put loose covers back on while they are still slightly damp as they will shrink to fit.

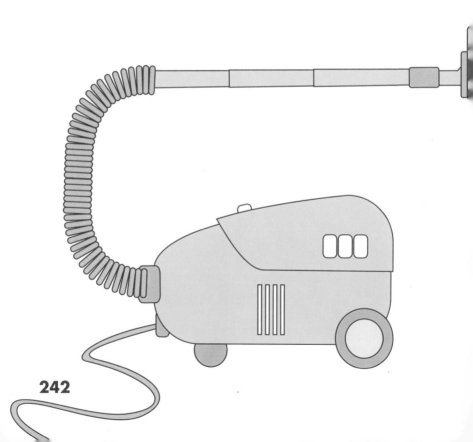

242

Feather Facts

• Plump cushions by shaking to re-distribute the filling and punching gently to get rid of dust.
• Don't plump too passionately as this can break up the feathers.
• Putting cushions out in the sunshine helps to fluff up the feathers.
• Beware – strong suction vacuuming can suck the feathers out !

bed advice

Take your bed apart from time to time and dust the frame thoroughly. Use a vacuum cleaner to remove dust and detritus from the mattress (don't forget to do both sides), padded headboards and divan bases. Turn the mattress over regularly according to the manufacturer's instructions.

Pro Antimacassar

How we laughed at dear old granny's antimacassars —
lace-edged or embroidered with crinoline ladies —
but today's heavy use of hairwax and gels suddenly
makes them seem like a good idea again. Avoid
embarassing stains and protect the backs of your
chairs and sofas.

5 alternative antimacassars

1 **cotton or woollen throw** – folded for neatness
2 **cotton dhurries** – the washable sort
3 **cotton or linen tablecloth** – lots to choose from
and easy to launder
4 **extra-large napkins** – buy a dozen and change
them frequently
5 **lace or embroidered crinoline ladies** – why
ever not?

To keep wicker and rattan soft and prevent it drying out treat it with vegetable oil (not extra-virgin, sunflower oil is thinner and cheaper). Put it on sparingly with a soft brush, rub it in and rub off any surplus with a soft cloth (taking care to avoid surface oil on areas that come into contact with clothes). Warming the oil thins it down making it easier to apply.

Wicker and Rattan

Dust collects in the weaves of wicker and rattan and soon turns to dirt if not removed. Dust frequently using a soft brush or vacuum cleaner with brush attachment. If it is very grubby wash with warm sudsy water, using a soft-bristled brush such as a toothbrush or washing-up brush to get into the nooks and crannies. Remove as much moisture as possible with a soft, dry cloth and then allow to dry naturally.

14 Precious Possessions

Treasures and precious objects deserve to be looked after, but they often require extra care to preserve both their looks and value. For antiques and collectors' items, it is best to seek and follow expert advice either from dealers or specialist books.

Retro Perspective

That junk-shop, carboot-sale, vintage or retro bargain often needs a good clean. Don't get carried away though, as over-cleaning can destroy not only the materials but also the character, and can even reduce the value.

Old laminates are more more vulnerable to damage: the edge trims are glued on so they will peel off if water gets into the joins. They are also less heat-resistant so be sure to use mats and trivets.

Do not use scourers or abrasives; clean with warm water and detergent and soften hardened-on dirt by soaking with a damp cloth. Pick out dirt from joins with a cocktail stick rather than a sharp metal object. Wipe down leatherette and vinyl with mild detergent and a damp cloth taking care to keep water out of seams, and dry thoroughly. As they are more prone to cracking and splitting keep away from radiators, heaters or bright sun.

Clean metal trims, legs and frames with the damp cloth treatment. Chrome finishes often have patches of rust; there is not much you can do except rub off any rough bits with the careful use of a soft scourer.

Antique Tips

When cleaning very expensive and valuable items, it is advisable to consult the experts, use specialist cleaning products or get them professionally treated and cleaned.

In the meantime, keep them well buffed and dutifully dusted.

• Keep precious furniture out of strong sunlight, which fades wood and fabrics. If this is impossible, turn furniture occasionally to ensure even fading and close curtains at times of maximum sun.

• Don't place hot, cold or wet objects directly on the surface. Use a mat.

• Central heating dries the atmosphere causing cracking, loose joints and warping. A humidifier maintains a constant level of humidity in the air, but placing a bowl of water in the room will also help to prevent wood from drying out.

• For general cleaning, use a duster or barely-damp cloth. Buff with a dry cloth to form a hard surface.

• Don't wax unnecessarily. Use a good-quality beeswax polish once or twice a year, polish sparingly, and preferably leave overnight, before buffing.

• Avoid aerosol spray polishes. They often contain silicon, which builds up a sticky surface, and a spirit, which removes natural oils in the wood.

• Don't clean metal handles with metallic cleaners as it will stain the surrounding wood, just give them a buffing.

Exquisite Accessories

Treat antique glass with care and never put it in a dishwasher. Likewise, the glazes on older ceramics may not be very stable and are almost certainly not dishwasherproof. Instead, wash them in warm, mild suds using a sponge or soft cloth; never scrub and accept that some marks cannot be removed.

To remove **tea and coffee stains** from pots put in a couple of heaped teaspoons (more for big pots and heavy staining) of **bicarbonate of soda** and top up with **warm water**, leave overnight and wash clean.

Clean out vases, jugs and decanters using the same method, but if something stronger is required use **vinegar** – rub it on or add water (1 part vinegar to 2 parts water) and leave to soak. Alternatively, if you have a couple of **denture tablets** drop them into a vase full of water overnight.

hand wash with care

It's always best to wash precious stuff by hand.
A plastic bowl has a soft surface, but washing directly in
the sink gives more room for manoeuvre. Either way,
put a cloth (one or two tea towels or a terry towel) in
the bottom to protect against damage and breakages.

• Get rid of loose, surface dust before washing.
• Use a gentle, colourless washing-up liquid.
• Wash in warm suds using a sponge or cloth and a
soft brush, such as a blusher brush, to get into
crevices and around handles. Do not rub too hard.
• Drain on a dish-drainer or draining board lined
with a towel or cloth.
• Leave to air dry or dry carefully with a clean, soft
tea towel or a hair-dryer on a warm setting.
• Gently buff up the surface with a soft cloth.

Precious Possessions

Silver Service

Solid silver is fairly soft so treat with care to avoid scratches and bashes. Silver-plate consists of a layer of silver on top of a cheaper, more robust metal. While good quality silver-plate has a relatively thick coating, inexpensive versions have a thin layer that gradually wears off with use and cleaning. The best way to keep silver looking good is to use it. Wash it in warm sudsy water, rinse well, dry and buff with a soft, lint-free cloth. Unused it will tarnish, unless stored away wrapped in acid-free tissue or non-dyed cotton or linen, which seems a shame.

Tarnish is caused by humidity so if you do keep it on display choose a dry environment and dust regularly using a soft brush. A quick buffing will deter tarnish build-up but it may be necessary to restore shine using a special silver cleaning product. As these products often remove a small amount of silver along with the tarnish it is best to eschew the liquid cleaners in favour of the impregnated cloths, which are gentler. For items with wooden knobs and handles be careful to keep the cleaning materials them as they can stain and damage the wood.

Bare hands and rubber
gloves will tarnish silver
so wear cotton gloves when
dusting and cleaning.

stainless steel and aluminium

These metals should not require anything more than dusting and a wipe over with a damp cloth from time to time. Small decorative items such as candlesticks or bowls and platters used for food should be washed in warm, sudsy water, rinsed and dried thoroughly. If some staining does occur try a paste of bicarbonate of soda or use a special proprietary product.

plastics and acrylics

Old plastics have become collectors' items and though plastic will not rust or tarnish it still needs to be cared for. The safest approach is to wipe down with a cloth dipped in mild detergent, rinse and buff up with a dry, soft cloth. Never use abrasives or scourers. Polish up the surface and remove fine scratches with metal polish. Finish off with an anti-static cloth.

wall hangings and textiles

As ever, dust is the enemy so keep as dust-free as possible either by shaking gently, brushing with a soft-bristled brush or using a vacuum cleaner on a low setting.

pictures and mirrors

• Don't hang valuable originals over a radiator or fireplace as the heat will damage them.
• Avoid damp walls and direct sunlight.
• Don't spray liquids directly onto glass as they can seep through to the picture or mirror and damage the frame or glass.
• Stop mirrors steaming up in bathrooms by rubbing with washing-up liquid and polishing with a clean soft cloth.

books

For precious books hold them closed and brush the edges of pages using a big make-up powder or blusher brush.

15 Electrical Equipment

Static electricity turns electrical equipment into a magnet for dust, which not only looks unsightly but can affect performance and efficiency over time.

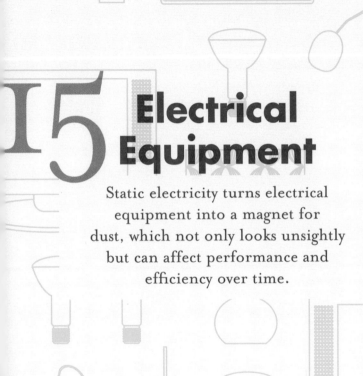

Lamps, Shades and Fittings

Dust loves lamps and light fittings where it often sits unnoticed. Don't forget to include fittings, lamps, shades and bases in your dusting routine.

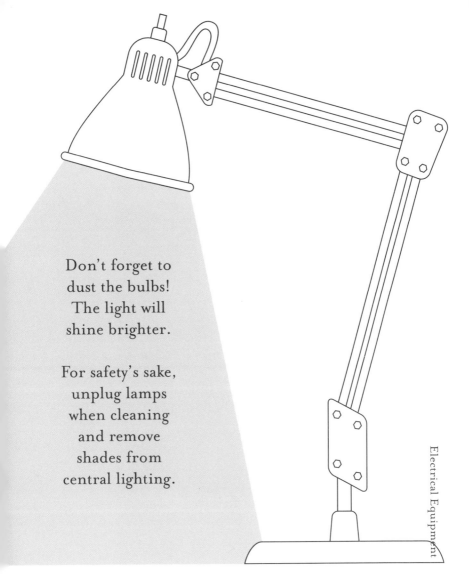

Don't forget to dust the bulbs! The light will shine brighter.

For safety's sake, unplug lamps when cleaning and remove shades from central lighting.

Shady Business

- The material used for a shade is often **glued** to the metal frame so therefore wetting is to be avoided.
- Hold **card shades** by the metal frame and dust gently with a very soft duster, brush or vacuum cleaner. Tackle dirty marks with an **eraser**, **white bread** or a **damp cloth**.
- Dust **fabric shades**, preferably with a vacuum cleaner, and use a proprietary spot cleaner on stains.
- Expensive **fabric shades** are sometimes sewn to the frame so they can be washed carefully in **warm sudsy water**. Rinse well — a gentle shower hose will force out more soap and dirt — shake off any excess water and gently blot off as much moisture as possible using a clean dry towel. Leave to dry, preferably in a sunny or breezy position.

• **Plastic shades** can be washed in **warm sudsy water**. Rinse, dry thoroughly and finish with a wipe over using an anti-static cloth.

• Wash **glass shades** in **warm sudsy water**, rinse and dry thoroughly.

• Dust **metal shades** and desk lamps thoroughly, wipe off marks with a **damp cloth** or for tougher dirt, rub with a cloth wrung out in **mild detergent** taking care not to splash any water into switches.

• **Chandeliers** will retain their sparkle if they are dusted frequently and occasionally washed in **warm sudsy water**. Wear **cotton gloves**; it's not only safer but keeps greasy fingermarks off the glass.

Computers +

Computers, music systems, TVs, videos and DVD players are often not the most attractive items and look even worse if they are dusty, discoloured and covered in finger marks.

- Clean fingermarks off **monitor screens** with a cloth dampened with **warm water** or proprietary **glass cleaner**.

- Do not use sprays **directly on monitors** and screens as they can cause damage.

- Remove marks from **casings** (but not keyboards) with a **damp cloth** or, where there is **discolouration**, a cloth dampened with **methylated spirit**.

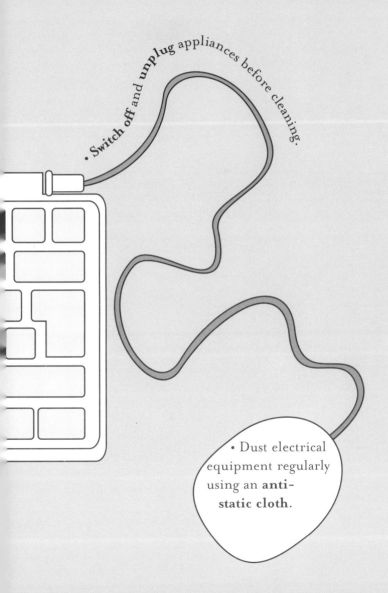

• **Switch off** and **unplug** appliances before cleaning.

• Dust electrical equipment regularly using an **anti-static cloth**.

Dust keyboards with a soft cloth, or feather duster, turn upside down to remove crumbs and use a small artist's paintbrush (or a photographic lens brush with puffer) to remove remaining fluff and stuff. Don't be tempted to blow out the dust and bits as the moisture in your breath could cause damage. If the brush doesn't get everything out use a can of compressed air, available from electronic shops and departments. You could also use a vacuum cleaner if you have a suitably soft brush attachment and low suction setting but read the manufacturer's instructions first.

Not only do computers and equipment attract dust they are often not the most attractive items in a room, so why not make jolly dust covers to complement the decor? If you are a whizz with the sewing machine make semi-fitted covers, otherwise, cover them with a small throw, attractive fabric or a gorgeous shawl.

Shock Tactics

There are a number of commercial anti-static treatments around, but here is a cheap and cheerful alternative to make yourself.

1 Soak a lint-free cloth in fabric softener diluted with water.
2 Squeeze out any excess liquid and allow to dry before use.
3 Treat two or three cloths at a time to ensure a good supply.

6 Pets' Corner

If you have a pet, it is important to keep your home as clean, sweet-smelling and allergen-free as possible. And the best place to start is with the animal concerned...

Pong Patrol

Animal owners love their pets to bits, but they are often unaware that their homes smell distinctly doggy or decidedly catty. As well as good grooming and rigorous cleaning routines, make sure there is plenty of ventilation to maintain a fresh atmosphere. Use natural products to scent or deodorise the home and don't use artificial air fresheners — even if they don't affect you, they may well harm your pet.

Good Grooming

• Regular grooming will not only make your pet less smelly but will also remove some of the dead skin and saliva flakes that cause allergies in humans.

• If possible groom your pet out-of-doors so that the hairs and flakes get blown away rather than just being re-distributed in the home.

• It isn't advisable to bath dogs more than once every 3 months as it can dry their skin and cause irritation. It isn't advisable to bath cats at all for your own safety!

• Provide pet bedding that is washable and wash it frequently. Washing at 60°C will kill bugs and any eggs from fleas.

• Tumble drying bedding will sterilise and get rid of pet hairs.
• If you allow pets on furniture and beds either protect them with a washable cover or wash the actual covers frequently.
• Vacuum and mop frequently around and underneath pet beds and their favourite places.
• A good vacuum cleaner will pick up most hairs from upholstery and carpets as long as you do it frequently, but a wipe over with a damp cloth may be more thorough.
• Blot up urine immediately. Rinse with vinegar solution, blot and dry.

Flea Pit

Fleas irritate pets. Not only do they carry potentially harmful diseases — the fleas on the rats actually carried the bubonic plague! — they cause itchy spots that can lead to serious skin problems. Fleas bite humans, too.

flea spotting

Fleas are dark brown and wriggle or jump, so look out for them when grooming your pets. They tend to live along the spine and around the neck, where you may also notice other small dark specks that are not flea eggs but droppings. If you manage to pick any fleas off your pet put them in a bowl of water otherwise they will hop off (or back on).

animal treatment

The vet is the best person to give advice and treatment. There are several ways of getting rid of fleas on your pet, including sprays, powders, flea collars, tablets and insecticidal liquids. Always follow the instructions carefully and don't use a product designed for one species on another — a dog product on a cat, for example.

home treatment

By treating your pet and your home, you will keep both free of fleas.

Wash your pet's bedding frequently. Unfortunately fleas lay their eggs away from animals so even if you rid the pet of fleas there are others hatching elsewhere ready to hop on and start all over again. Using a powder or spray at frequent intervals over a period of time will help break the cycle. Spray bedding, chair and floor coverings concentrating along the edges of carpets and skirting boards – and don't forget to put some in the vacuum cleaner bag. As with any insecticides these sprays and powders are potentially harmful if breathed in or ingested so use carefully and follow the instructions. Tropical fish and small children are particularly vulnerable and any food should be covered to avoid contamination. If problems persist and you suspect you have an infestation, call in the experts who will treat your home efficiently and safely.

Words on Worms

Even the best-loved and pampered pets can get worms and as they can cause distress and ill-health they must be dealt with. There may be no obvious signs but look out for worms in their vomit, poo and around their nether regions. There are two kinds of worm: roundworm and tapeworm.

roundworms

Roundworms are spread from animal to animal, they look like very thin, pale earthworms. They can be passed on to humans if the eggs are accidentally ingested. Often this is from the fingers or from plates that pets have licked or from the soil.

tapeworms

A tapeworm is a long flat worm made up of segments with a head that attaches itself to the intestine. Mature segments break away and can be seen in the poo or around the base of the tail; they look like grains of rice that, rather alarmingly, can be seen to move. Tapeworms in dogs are often spread by fleas and in cats by fleas, mice, shrews and voles, but they can also be picked up from uncooked meat.

treatment

It is always best to consult a vet as he or she will offer professional advice and prescribe the correct dosage for your pet. Professionally administered or prescribed treatments tend to be more effective, but licensed roundworm and tapeworm remedies are also available from a pharmacist, pet shop or supermarket. Always follow the manufacturer's instructions and keep all medicines away from children.

Most worms will not normally affect humans, but there are a few that can cause severe illness so it makes sense to be vigilant and ensure that there is no poo or traces of poo in the house. Check your pet's bottom and the surrounding fur or hair regularly and be prepared to wipe or wash if necessary.

Clean out cat litter every day and be a good citizen and pick up and dispose of your dog's faeces so that no unsuspecting person or child will come into contact with it.

17

PS

Daily chores can be a bore, but a
traditional Spring clean will almost
certainly raise your spirits and that of
your home. You may find that reviving
a tired-looking interior involves
nothing more than a good dose of TLC.
If, however, you are more desperate
housewife than perfect homemaker,
there is no shame in getting someone in
to keep your home in the condition to
which you wish to become accustomed.

Quick Transformation

Sometimes, people mistake the need for redecoration with the need for a good clean, so if redecorating doesn't fill you with enthusiasm or is just not an option, you can still transform a room using all the cleaning tips in this book plus a few changes.

clean

- clean windows inside and out
- get rid of dust from all surfaces including walls, window and door frames
- wash down grubby paintwork and walls and tackle stains and dirt around light switches, door handles and skirting boards
- wash down work surfaces
- dust / wipe down appliances
- dust / wipe down electrical equipment
- dust blinds and wash or wipe clean
- wash or freshen up curtains, covers, throws, cushion covers etc.
- vacuum upholstery, clean and freshen up as necessary
- vacuum floors thoroughly, including carpets and rugs
- freshen up carpet if necessary
- give floors a good mop or scrub

clean +

- change the furniture round
- paint one wall a trendy colour
- put up new pictures
- change the cushion covers

The Big Clean

A major clear-out and a clean-up is good for the soul and most homes will benefit from such activities at least once or twice a year. Even if you are the dutiful housewife type there will be some top shelf with a vestige of dirt, and if you are a slob this provides an opportunity to salvage your reputation.

The actual cleaning methods are much the same as for normal daily or weekly chores, but the big clean involves being much more thorough, getting underneath everything and into every nook, cranny, corner and crevice.

be prepared

• **Set aside** plenty of time to do things properly, two days is ideal — aim to start early the first morning and finish the following afternoon leaving the evening free for a celebratory meal in the newly pristine environment.

• **Send** children, cleanaphobic partners, pets and lazy housemates to stay with relatives or friends in order to ensure that they don't get in the way, fall over things or demand gourmet meals despite the fact that the kitchen has been turned upside down and the cooker is in pieces.

• **Check** you have ample supplies of cleaning materials, implements, cloths and sponges.

• **Stock up** on plenty of big bin liners handy for rubbish, re-cycling and stuff for the charity shop.

• **Be aware** of health and safety and get in a good supply of rubber gloves (including heavy-duty ones) and face masks to protect from excess dust or cleaning sprays and fumes.

• **Protect** valuable items and flooring by using large dust sheets.

• **Test** your step-ladder, which you will need to get to high shelves, light fittings and tops of cupboards, to make sure it is in good order and safe to use.

• **Empty** the vacuum cleaner and make sure it is in good working order.

• **Reward** yourself for your hard work with a plentiful supply of treats. This is an opportunity to indulge in naughty-but-nice stuff such as crisps, biscuits, chocolate and cake.

PS

Getting Someone In

If, despite all efforts you can't, or won't, clean your home and as a result are losing face and friends it's time to get someone in to do it for you. Cleaning is not just for Christmas it's for life, but while some are born to clean others have cleanliness thrust upon them. However, few would dispute the fact that a clean home is more pleasant to live in so if cleaning is not for you why not consider paying someone to do it for you?

The Search

Finding someone to come and 'do' for you is not always easy. Personal recommendation is preferable so ask friends and neighbours first. If nothing turns up try an agency or place an advert in the local press or in a shop window – don't give your address, just a telephone number (preferably a mobile).

references

Request references from previous employers and don't be afraid to follow them up, anyone who is any good won't mind. In the case of written references a quick telephone call will confirm that they are genuine and weren't written with a loaded mop held to the writer's head.

interview

The chances are that someone who takes no pride whatsoever in their appearance is unlikely to care much about the appearance of your home, but it's not always the case. However, long painted nails suggest an unwillingness to get stuck in and whereas dirty nails may imply the opposite they may also indicate a lack of attention to detail. Don't be afraid to use your gut instincts when judging potential applicants, remember, you will be handing over your front door key so trust is imperative.

Don't spring clean the house before interviewing a cleaner — it may make you feel good but it won't offer any insight into what the actual job entails.

The Good Employer

Take your new cleaner round the house and agree on a basic set of tasks and, if necessary, establish whether he/she is willing to be flexible, for example tackling ironing one week or giving the spare room a good going over the next. Make clear any 'house rules' or 'no-go areas', not forgetting to explain the security and alarm systems.

Cleaners are easily offended especially if they arrive to find 'keep out' signs and padlocks on the cupboards so if you have particularly valuable items lock them away discreetly.

If you own a lot of precious furniture and objects either check they know how to care for them properly (you don't want that Ming vase put in the dishwasher and neither do you want your delightfully dilapidated look given a character assassination with over-zealous cleaning), or declare them off-limits with cleaning duties restricted to the basics.

Don't feel you have to clean before the cleaner comes but it is polite to tidy up – remember you are employing a cleaner not a lady's maid.

Be nice to your cleaner and always pay promptly. Establish boundaries early on – it's a good idea to forbid them bringing anyone else such as children or friends into the house, and don't give them free range of the fridge as you could come home to find your favourite chocolate or tonight's dinner gratefully consumed, best to leave a tray attractively laid out with tea and coffee-making facilities plus, to show your appreciation, a few up-market biscuits.

Keep the relationship professional; cleaners can too easily become a best friend or a tyrant, neither of which is desirable. Remember, you are the boss. It's difficult to complain that the bath isn't clean if you've just shared your innermost secrets over coffee.

Keeping Your Cleaner Equipped

Once you have found your cleaner you may be shocked when they demand a better class of vacuum cleaner and insist that you stock their favourite cleaning materials. However, be warned, bicarbonate of soda and vinegar are rarely on their list, instead you may be asked to buy new (and expensive) wonder cleaning products – the sort that can destroy surfaces, your health and eventually the planet. So if you feel strongly about such things, you may have be prepared to compromise (with branded, basic, proprietary products) rather than risk losing a good cleaner.

useful addresses

general cleaning products and tools

John Lewis
www.johnlewis.com

Labour and Wait
www.labourandwait.co.uk

Lakeland Limited
www.lakelandlimited.com

eco-friendly cleaning products

WWF Earthly Goods Online Store
www.wwf.org.uk

MyPure
www.mypure.co.uk

EcoEstates
www.ecoestates.co.uk

Goodness Direct
www.goodnessdirect.uk

Natural Collection
www.naturalcollection.com

organisations and advisory bodies

Good Housekeeping Institute
www.goodhousekeeping.co.uk

Greenpeace (The Chemical Home)
www.greenpeace.org.uk

British Veterinary Association
www.bva.co.uk

Department of Health
www.dh.gov.uk

index

acknowledgements

Thanks to the Quadrille team: Jane O'Shea, the enthusiastic editorial director, Lisa Pendreigh the perfect editor, and Claire Peters, the adventurous designer.

304